THE MANGANARO
ITALIAN FAMILY COOKBOOK

THE MANGANARO ITALIAN FAMILY COOKBOOK

SELINE DELL'ORTO

Edited by
Linda Foley Woodrum

Illustrated by Susan Edison.
Book designed by Deborah Jackson-Jones.

Library of Congress Cataloging-in-Publication Data

Dell'Orto, Seline.
    The Manganaro Italian family cookbook / Seline Dell'Orto.
        p.   cm.
    Includes index.
    ISBN 0-9655800-0-8 : $19.95
    1. Cookery, Italian.   I. Title.
TX723.D397   1989
641.5945—dc20   89-30441
                                                 CIP

Printed in the United States of America

10 9 8 7 6 5 4 3 2

To my father and mother,
my sisters Linda, Nina, Marissa, and Lisa,
and our many loyal customers.

CONTENTS

—————— **ACKNOWLEDGMENTS** ——————

I want to thank Linda Woodrum, with whom it has been a joy to work, and my grandmothers D'Angelo and Dell'Orto, who have taught me what great Italian cooking should be.

INTRODUCTION

When you walk into our store, Manganaro Foods, you take a step back in time. Worn but spotless wooden floors creak beneath your feet while imported ham, cheeses, and provoletti hang from the rafters over your head. And, aahhh, the aroma. Your nose will tell you you're in the right place!

I guess what amazes me the most is that even though our business has grown over the years, it's basically still the same store that my great-uncle started years ago. The rich, colorful history attached to this store and this neighborhood will help you understand what Manganaro Foods and our family are all about.

How We Began

Manganaro Foods was established in 1910 when my great-uncle, James Manganaro, made his way from Italy to New York. He came to work for his uncle, Ernest Petrucci, who had owned and operated Petrucci's Wine and Liquor store on Ninth Avenue since 1893. In 1914 Great-uncle James was drafted, but he returned to the store after his military service. Soon, James decided to open an imported Italian food shop two blocks from his uncle's liquor store. When Prohibition took effect, James moved his food operation to his uncle's store—our present location at 488 Ninth Avenue, New York, New York.

How We Grew

Manganaro Foods flourished, and eventually Uncle James was joined by his brother, Louis. In the early 1920s they sent for their sister, Nina (my grandmother), and mother, Michaela (my great-grandmother). It was during these early years that the Ninth Avenue neighborhood was known as Hell's Kitchen. As its name suggested, it was a pretty rough area, inhabited mainly by Irish and Italian immigrants.

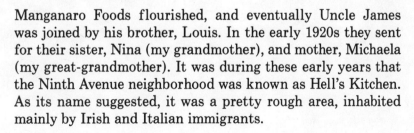

Seline's great-aunts and uncles, circa 1880

The Manganaro Italian Family Cookbook

But the character of the area didn't hurt the Manganaro business. In fact, the store was a popular gathering spot for opera stars. Back then, the Metropolitan Opera was located near the store. Uncle James couldn't have been happier—he loved the opera! All of the opera performers would descend upon Manganaro Foods to refuel their creative talents with great Italian food, and, as Uncle James soon discovered, opera stars have very healthy appetites!

Soon it was time to start a family so the traditions brought over from Italy could be carried on. In 1924 my grandmother, Nina Manganaro, married my grandfather, Anthony Dell'Orto. They lived above the store and became the proud parents of four healthy sons, one of whom became my father, Sal. As Sal grew up, he and his brother, Vincent, were a major part of the family venture.

In 1949 my father, Sal Dell'Orto, married my mother, Marion D'Angelo. In no time at all they had five daughters, of whom I am the eldest. I remember growing up around the store and getting in everyone's way. I loved the smell of the fresh imported cheeses and sausages. I would watch my father for

Manganaro's, circa 1920

hours as he sliced meat paper-thin and made sandwiches for hungry customers. I would patiently wait for him to give me a sandwich (which he never did). He was the all-time best sandwich maker. He still is.

It wasn't until I was sixteen or seventeen years old that I began working at the store. Like everyone else who starts at Manganaro's I was assigned first to the kitchen, making sandwiches and salads. Soon I graduated to hot foods and eventually worked behind the front counter. It was a good training process and prepared me well for running the business today.

Seline's grandmother Dell'Orto and James Manganaro (on the left), circa 1925

The Manganaro Italian Family Cookbook

Our Changing Menu ———————— 🫛

Our customers are willing to try all kinds of different foods. My favorite part of this business is making a new, special dish so I can listen to everyone tell me how delicious it is! I make it a point to change our menu according to the seasons. In the spring we serve many fresh vegetables, veal and lamb. In the summer we offer our customers pesto, fresh mozzarella, and plump tomatoes. Fall usually means Pasta Fagioli and Minestrone, and in the winter we dish out plenty of hearty polenta and potato dishes.

Manganaro's, circa 1925

Manganaro's, circa 1950

Seline's grandmother Dell'Orto and her brother

Seline and her father, Sal Dell'Orto

The Manganaro Italian Family Cookbook

Since Manganaro Foods was founded, our neighborhood has undergone many changes. In the early 1940s, construction on the Lincoln tunnel forced thousands of families to move from the area. In the late 1950s and early 1960s, many people packed up and headed for the suburbs.

Despite all the transitions, Manganaro's is still a thriving family business. You can stop in almost anytime and see that there is mass confusion, but we're having fun. My father usually opens the store every morning at 8:00, and on good days I arrive between 9:30 and 11:00. My first priority is to make myself a cappuccino. Then I walk around and make everyone laugh before I get down to business.

Besides my father and me, my sisters, Linda, Nina, Marissa, and Lisa help out whenever they can. Of course, it's a little crazy when we are all there contributing our talents, but it's great fun.

We're a proud family and we are working hard to carry on Great-uncle James's dream. In the years to come I hope I am doing the same thing, only better. (My second choice is to move to a sunny, beautiful beach somewhere in Mexico.)

We've been at 488 Ninth Avenue for a long time and intend to be here for a lot longer. So if you're ever in New York on Ninth Avenue between Thirty-seventh and Thirty-eighth Streets, stop by and say hello. We would love to meet you and serve you some of our delicious Italian food.

Buen Appetito!

Seline Dell'Orto

HOLIDAY MENUS

Thanksgiving Dinner

We give thanks every year for our family of good cooks! As you can see by this menu, we have plenty to be thankful for. We usually spend the day cooking and nibbling on appetizers. When it is time for the main meal, we always turn it into a two-hour extravaganza.

⋅§ Baked Clams ᡠ⋅

Shrimp Cocktail

Dried Sausage

Fresh Mozzarella Cheese

Marinated Fresh Fennel

⋅§ Marinated Mushrooms ᡠ⋅

⋅§ Chicken and Tortellini Soup ᡠ⋅

⋅§ Lasagna ᡠ⋅

Cranberry Sauce

⋅§ Stuffed Artichokes ᡠ⋅

Baked Sweet Potatoes

⋅§ Radicchio Salad ᡠ⋅

⋅§ Sauteed Mushrooms ᡠ⋅

⋅§ Baked Apples and Yams ᡠ⋅

⋅§ Stuffed Turkey ᡠ⋅

⋅§ Pumpkin Pie ᡠ⋅

Pecan Pie

Apple Pie

Ice Cream

⋅§ These recipes appear in the book. Check the index for the page numbers.

Christmas Eve Dinner

*T*his is our big holiday meal. My mother spends hours in the kitchen preparing for this feast, although we all help her out. We keep with the Italian tradition of eating only fish on Christmas Eve. For Christmas Day, we simply prepare a roast and eat the leftovers from Christmas Eve. After midnight we make sausage and ricotta heros and baked figs with bacon.

Antipasto

Fried Smelts

Bread Sticks

Baked Clams

Shrimp Cocktail

Lobster in Red Sauce

White Clam Sauce

Steamed Vegetables

Romaine and Blue Cheese Salad

Assorted Chocolates

Honey Balls

Popcorn Balls

Almond Cookies

Fruitcake

Creamed Spinach

Palm Sunday Brunch

*E*very year on Palm Sunday my family goes to church and then rushes over to my mother's house for this special banquet.

Assorted Fruit Juices

Champagne

Halved Grapefruit

Bagels

Cream Cheese

Lox

Assorted Jellies

Butter

Cinnamon Buns

Danish

Coffee Cake

Italian Breakfast Sausage (Luganega)

Bacon

Virginia Ham Slices

Hash

French Fries

Pancakes

Frittatas

Easter Dinner

*E*aster is the day for our annual family reunion. Everyone gathers at my grandmother's house to eat and have a good time. We adhere to the same family traditions every year. For instance, we always end the Easter meal with Lasagna.

Assorted Olives

Roasted Peppers

Bread Sticks

Dried Sausage

Sicilian Easter Soup (Shesheddu)

Stuffed Turkey

Roast Beef

Fried Vegetables

Eggplant Parmesan

Stuffed Mushrooms

Romaine and Blue Cheese Salad

Steamed Broccoli with Cheese

Italian Meatballs

Steamed Asparagus

Lasagna

Honey Balls

Assorted Cakes

Fresh Fruit

Assorted Cheeses

Happy Birthday Celebration

We celebrated a friend's fortieth birthday with this feast at our store. Fifty hungry people came and fifty stuffed party goers left.

Mascarpone on Angel Toast
Deviled Eggs
Neapolitan Rice Balls (Miniature)
Italian Meatballs
Olives
Paté
Assorted Cheeses
Eggplant Rollatini
Sauteed Mushrooms
Bacon-Wrapped Shrimp
Garlic Scallops with Sun-Dried Tomatoes
Baked Clams
Baked Ziti
Eggplant Salad
Tortellini Salad
Birthday Cake
Assorted Cookies

New Year's Day Dinner

We keep this menu very light. After ringing in the New Year the night before, no one wants to eat a huge meal.

Chicken and Tortellini Soup
Virginia Baked Ham
Baked Sweet Potatoes
Peas
Steamed Vegetables
Stringbean and Tomato Salad
Fresh Fruit
Assorted Cakes

APPETIZERS

At our house, appetizers mean a celebration. We make the recipes in this chapter for big parties, birthday dinners, or holiday festivities. We can always think of a reason to celebrate, so appetizers are a familiar part of our cooking.

Some recipes, such as Baked Clams or Chicken Wings, are easy to prepare, while others, such as Spedini, take more time but are worth every minute. Try one or try them all. Most importantly, have fun at your next party!

Stuffed Mushrooms

20 large mushrooms
1   small onion, finely chopped
¼   cup chopped parsley
¼   cup olive oil
1 ½ cups dry bread crumbs
½   cup grated Parmesan cheese
¼   teaspoon salt
¼   teaspoon pepper

To dress up this recipe, add 1 pound of chopped fresh shrimp to the filling. Cook the chopped shrimp in the skillet with the mushroom stems, onion, and parsley.

Clean mushrooms and remove stems. Chop stems. In a large skillet cook mushroom stems, onion, and parsley in oil till onion is tender. Stir in bread crumbs, Parmesan cheese, salt, and pepper. Arrange mushrooms in a shallow baking pan. Spoon cheese mixture into mushroom caps. Bake in a 350°F oven for 15 minutes or till mushrooms are tender and cheese mixture is heated through.

Makes 10 appetizer servings.

Chicken Wings

12 chicken wings (about 2 pounds)
⅓   cup soy sauce
2   tablespoons sugar
2   tablespoons applesauce
5   cloves garlic, finely chopped

Aunt Rose makes this appetizer for the children to eat before dinner. Plan on 2 to 4 wings per person, depending on what other appetizers you serve.

Rinse chicken; pat dry with paper towels. Place chicken wings in a large plastic bag. Set bag in a bowl. For marinade, stir together soy sauce, sugar, applesauce, and garlic. Pour over chicken wings in bag. Seal bag. Place chicken wings in the refrigerator and marinate for 4 hours or overnight, turning bag occasionally.

Drain chicken wings and arrange in a shallow baking pan. Bake in a 375°F oven for 1 hour. Broil for the last few minutes, until chicken wings are brown and crisp.

Makes 3 to 6 appetizer servings.

Mussels in Olive Oil

To make this easy recipe into a main dish, serve it with 1 pound of linguine.

36   **fresh mussels in shells**
4   **quarts cold water**
⅓   **cup salt**
11   **cloves garlic, chopped**
1 ½ **cups olive oil**
1   **cup chopped parsley**
1   **teaspoon salt**
1   **teaspoon crushed red pepper**

Scrub mussels under cold running water. Pull out the beards that are visible between the shells. In a dutch oven combine cold water and ⅓ cup salt. Add mussels. Soak for 15 minutes; drain and rinse. Repeat soaking, draining, and rinsing twice.

In the same dutch oven cook garlic in oil till tender but not brown. Add mussels, parsley, 1 teaspoon salt, and red pepper. Bring to boiling; reduce heat. Cover and simmer about 5 minutes or till shells open. Discard any shells that do not open. Serve with lots of bread for dipping.

Makes 12 appetizer servings.

 ## Clams and Mussels

Clams come in two varieties: hard- and soft-shell. Common hard-shell clams include the Atlantic quahog and the Pacific littleneck, geoduck, and razor clam. Clams of the soft-shell variety have necks that stick out of the shells. When buying fresh clams, make sure the clam is alive by tapping the shell. If the clam is alive, the shell on the hard-shell clam will close and the neck on the soft-shell clam will move. When buying shucked clams, choose ones that are plump with clear juices. You can store live clams in the refrigerator up to 2 days.

Mussels have bluish-black shells with a tender, smoky-tasting meat inside. As with clams, select live mussels that close when tapped. You can store live mussels in the refrigerator up to 2 days.

Baked Clams

12 **clams in shells**
¾ **cup dry bread crumbs**
½ **cup olive oil**
¼ **cup chopped parsley**
3 **garlic cloves, finely chopped**
½ **teaspoon salt**
½ **teaspoon pepper**

This is my favorite way to prepare fresh clams. If you like clams, I believe you'll love this recipe.

Open clams; remove clam muscle. Reserve clam juice and half of the shells. Scrub shells under cold running water and place in a single layer in a shallow baking pan.

In a mixing bowl stir together bread crumbs, oil, parsley, garlic powder, salt, and pepper. Place 1 clam in each shell in baking pan. Spoon bread crumb mixture over clams. Bake, uncovered, in a 375°F oven for 15 to 20 minutes or till brown.

Makes 6 appetizer servings.

Fried Codfish (Baccala)

1 **pound salted, dried codfish**
1 **cup flour**
2 **tablespoons grated Parmesan cheese**
1 **teaspoon pepper**
¼ **teaspoon salt**
¼ **teaspoon garlic powder**
½ **cup water**
2 **cups olive oil**

Codfish is very salty and needs to be soaked in water for 3 days before using. When you taste the results, you'll know it's worth the effort.

Place codfish in a large bowl. Cover with water. Cover and soak in the refrigerator for three days, changing water each day.

In a mixing bowl stir together flour, cheese, pepper, salt, and garlic powder. Add water. Stir till well combined.

Dip each piece of codfish in batter. Fry in hot oil for 2 minutes per side or till golden brown. Drain on paper towels.

Makes 8 to 10 appetizer servings.

Fried Smelts

My sister Nina thinks it's great fun to eat these whole, crisply-fried fish as appetizers. We usually nibble on them on Christmas Eve.

24 medium-sized whole smelts (about 2 pounds)
6   eggs, beaten
½   cup milk
½   teaspoon salt
½   teaspoon pepper
4   cups flour
2   cups olive oil

Rinse smelts; pat dry with paper towels. In a mixing bowl combine eggs, milk, salt, and pepper. Dip smelts in egg mixture. Coat with flour. Fry in hot oil for 3 to 4 minutes per side or till golden brown. Drain on paper towels. If desired, dip in marinara sauce.

Makes 8 appetizer servings.

 ## Beer-Batter Vegetables

Some of our favorite vegetables to deep-fry are fresh mushrooms, cauliflower and broccoli pieces, onion rings, and green pepper strips.

2   cups flour
1   package active dry yeast
⅛   teaspoon salt
⅛   teaspoon pepper
4   eggs, beaten
1   12-ounce can cold beer
2   tablespoons olive oil
5   cups vegetables
4   cups olive oil

In a mixing bowl stir together flour, yeast, salt, and pepper. Add eggs, beer, and 2 tablespoons oil. Stir till smooth. Let stand at room temperature for 1 hour.

Pat vegetables dry with paper towels. Dip vegetables in beer batter. In a heavy saucepan, fry vegetables, a few at a time, in deep hot oil (375°F) for 2 to 3 minutes or till golden brown. Drain on paper towels.

Makes 8 appetizer servings.

Fried Chicken Nuggets

2 ½ **pounds boneless, skinless chicken breasts**
2 **cups flour**
2 **cups grated Parmesan cheese**
½ **teaspoon salt**
½ **teaspoon pepper**
2 **tablespoons dried oregano, crushed**
2 **cups dry bread crumbs**
½ **cup milk**
2 **eggs, beaten**
4 **cups cooking oil**

This recipe comes from our good friend, J. R. He suggests serving these bite-size pieces of fried chicken with purchased honey mustard.

Rinse chicken; pat dry with paper towels, and cut into bite-size pieces. In a plastic bag combine flour, Parmesan cheese, salt, pepper, and oregano. In another bag place bread crumbs. Put half of the chicken pieces in bag with flour mixture. Close bag and shake to coat. Stir together milk and eggs. Dip chicken in egg mixture. Transfer chicken to bag with bread crumbs. Close bag and shake to coat. Repeat with remaining chicken.

Fry chicken pieces in hot oil about 2 minutes or until golden brown. Drain on paper towels.

Makes 6 to 8 appetizer servings.

 ## Fried Appetizers

For the best results when you deep-fat fry appetizers, keep these hints in mind.

⤷ Choose a heavy skillet or large saucepan that is at least 3 inches deep. Or, use an electric deep-fat fryer or a wok.

⤷ If you have a deep-fat thermometer, use it to help you keep track of the oil temperature. The best temperature for frying foods is 375°F. If the temperature of the oil is too low, the food will be greasy, and if it's too high, the food will burn before it cooks.

⤷ Add food to the hot oil a little at a time. Adding too much food at once will lower the oil temperature.

Fried Vegetables

This recipe for fried vegetables is milder and a little fancier than the Beer-Batter Vegetables.

5   eggs
½   cup milk
½   teaspoon salt
½   teaspoon pepper
1   9-ounce package frozen artichoke hearts, thawed
1   10-ounce package frozen cut asparagus, thawed
1   10-ounce package frozen cut cauliflower, thawed
1   medium zucchini, sliced
4   cups dry bread crumbs
2   cups olive oil

In a mixing bowl stir together eggs, milk, salt, and pepper. Pat vegetables dry with paper towels. Dip vegetables in egg mixture. Coat with bread crumbs. In a heavy saucepan fry vegetables, a few at a time, in hot oil (375°F) for 2 to 4 minutes or till golden brown. Drain on paper towels.

Makes 12 appetizer servings.

 Spedini

These special-occasion appetizers are thin pieces of veal rolled around a seasoned breadcrumb filling. They're perfect for large parties.

1   large onion, chopped
⅔   cup olive oil
3   cups dry bread crumbs
½   cup grated Romano cheese
2   tablespoons chopped parsley
½   teaspoon salt
½   teaspoon pepper
2   pounds veal cutlets, cut into 20 strips
1   cup olive oil
1   small onion, broken into large pieces
8 to 10   bay leaves
          Olive oil

In a large skillet cook the large onion in ⅔ cup oil till tender. Stir in bread crumbs, Romano cheese, and parsley. Season with salt and pepper. Remove from heat.

To assemble veal rolls, dip veal in 1 cup olive oil. Spoon bread crumb mixture over one side of the veal. Roll up veal around filling. Secure with wooden toothpicks, if necessary. Arrange stuffed veal rolls, seam side down, on a greased baking sheet. Arrange the pieces of the small onion and bay leaves on and around veal. Brush lightly with olive oil. Bake, uncovered, in a 375°F oven for 20 to 30 minutes or till veal is tender and golden brown. Serve warm.

Makes 20 appetizer servings.

 Christmas Champagne

1   **3-ounce package lime-flavored gelatin**
Fresh or thawed, frozen whole strawberries
Champagne

Toast the holidays with this festive red and green bubbly.

Prepare lime-flavored gelatin according to package directions. For each serving, place 3 strawberries in a stemmed glass. Place 1 spoonful of lime-flavored gelatin in the glass with the strawberries. Fill with champagne.

SOUPS

Soups have a magical way of making people feel warm and cozy inside. That's why they're perfect for cooler weather. Our store has proof of this: we serve soups by the gallon when it's cold outside.

Most of the soups in this chapter are offered at our store; the most popular are Minestrone, Fagioli Soup, and Lentil and Escarole Soup. Whether we serve them with a sandwich or salad, our customers never seem to tire of these steaming bowls of goodness. You can make the soups which call for pasta with any pasta shape you like.

Lentil and Escarole Soup

8   cups water
1   pound dry lentils
¼   cup olive oil
4   stalks celery, diced
4   cloves garlic, whole
3   heads escarole, torn
½   teaspoon salt
¼   teaspoon pepper
1   cup grated Parmesan Cheese

In a large saucepan or dutch oven, bring water, lentils, oil, celery, and garlic to a boil. Reduce heat.

Simmer, uncovered, for 1 hour or till lentils are soft. Add escarole, salt, and pepper; remove from heat. Serve with grated Parmesan cheese.

Makes 8 servings.

Rice and Lentil Soup

1   medium onion, chopped
4   cloves garlic, finely chopped
4   quarts water
1   pound dry lentils, rinsed
2   cups Arborio or long grain rice
5   stalks celery, sliced
4   carrots, chopped
½   teaspoon salt
½   teaspoon pepper
¼   teaspoon garlic powder

For a colorful combination, you can add 1 pound of fresh spinach to this soup along with the lentils.

In a dutch oven cook onion and garlic in oil till onion is tender. Add water, lentils, rice, celery, carrots, salt, pepper, and garlic powder. Bring to boiling; reduce heat.

Simmer, uncovered, for 1½ hours or till rice and lentils are tender, stirring occasionally.

Makes 8 servings.

Sicilian Easter Soup

Also known as Shesheddu, this traditional Easter Sunday soup recipe was developed by my grandmother. As far as we know, her recipe is unique.

1	2 ½ to 3 pound chicken, cut up
8	cups water
1	pound beef stew meat
1	medium onion, cut into wedges
6	carrots, sliced long
4	stalks celery, sliced long
½	bunch parsley
1	teaspoon salt
1	teaspoon celery seed
1	teaspoon onion powder
½	teaspoon pepper
½	teaspoon garlic powder
3	slices bread
2	eggs, beaten
1	pound ground beef
1	cup grated Parmesan cheese
3	tablespoons dried parsley
1	teaspoon pepper
½	teaspoon garlic powder
½	teaspoon celery seed
½	teaspoon onion powder
1	pound ricotta cheese
5	eggs
1	cup grated Parmesan cheese

For the chicken broth, in a dutch oven combine chicken, 8 cups water, beef stew meat, onion, carrots, celery, parsley, 1 teaspoon salt, 1 teaspoon celery seed, 1 teaspoon onion powder, ½ teaspoon pepper, and ½ teaspoon garlic powder. Bring to boiling; reduce heat.

Simmer, uncovered, for 1½ hours. Lift out chicken pieces and beef with a slotted spoon.

To strain, pour broth through a colander or sieve lined with 2 layers of cheesecloth. Discard vegetables and seasonings.

When cool enough to handle, remove chicken from bones and shred. Shred beef. Discard bones. Return chicken and beef to broth mixture.

For meatballs, cover bread with warm water and soak for 2 minutes or till soft. Drain and squeeze out excess water. In a mixing bowl combine the 2 eggs, ground beef, soaked bread,

Parmesan cheese, parsley, 1 teaspoon pepper, ½ teaspoon garlic powder, ½ teaspoon celery seed, and ½ teaspoon onion powder. Mix well. Form meat mixture into ½-inch meatballs. Set aside. In another mixing bowl stir together ricotta cheese and the 5 eggs. Set aside.

Bring broth and meat mixture to boiling. Add meatballs. Return to boiling; reduce heat. Simmer, uncovered, for 30 minutes. Add ricotta mixture, 1 tablespoon at a time, to boiling mixture. Continue to simmer for 3 minutes more or till ricotta mixture rises to the top. Sprinkle with 1 cup grated Parmesan cheese before serving. Serve with additional grated Parmesan cheese, if desired.

Makes 24 servings.

 ## Capellini and Sausage Soup

1	pound bulk pork sausage
1	large onion, chopped
8	cups water
1	pound fresh green beans, trimmed
2	cups trimmed brussels sprouts
1	head cauliflower, cut into bite-size pieces
8	ounces fresh mushrooms
2	medium tomatoes, cut into wedges
1	16-ounce can whole white potatoes, drained
1	16-ounce can peas, drained
1	teaspoon salt
½	teaspoon pepper
¼	teaspoon dried tarragon, crushed
1	pound capellini (angel hair pasta)
½	cup grated Parmesan cheese

We like to begin our football tailgate parties with a huge batch of this vegetable-studded soup.

In a dutch oven cook sausage and onion till sausage is brown and onion is tender. Add water, green beans, brussels sprouts, cauliflower, mushrooms, tomatoes, potatoes, peas, salt, pepper, and tarragon. Bring to boiling; reduce heat.

Simmer, uncovered, for 45 minutes. Add capellini. Return to boiling; reduce heat. Simmer for 10 minutes more or till pasta is al dente. Serve with grated Parmesan cheese.

Makes 8 servings.

Cream of Artichoke Soup

I call this "Malibu Soup" because that's where my sister Linda created this recipe.

4	medium potatoes, diced
3	stalks celery, finely chopped
3	medium carrots, diced
1	medium onion, finely chopped
½	cup butter or margarine
8	cups milk
1	teaspoon salt
½	teaspoon pepper
3	14-ounce cans artichoke hearts
¼	cup cream sherry

In a large saucepan cook potatoes, celery, carrots and onion in butter till vegetables are tender. Stir in milk, salt, and pepper. Bring to boiling; reduce heat. Simmer, uncovered, for 15 minutes.

Meanwhile, place undrained artichoke hearts in a blender container or food processor bowl. Cover and blend or process till smooth. Add to saucepan. Cook and stir for 5 minutes. Add sherry. Heat through.

Makes 8 to 10 servings.

 ## Pasta and Fagioli Soup

This bean soup is flavored with prosciutto and garlic.

1	pound dry cannellini beans
6	cups water
4	stalks celery, sliced
8	ounces prosciutto or Canadian bacon, chopped
5	cloves garlic, whole
2	tablespoons olive oil
1	teaspoon salt
½	teaspoon pepper
1	pound tubetti pasta

Place dry beans in a colander or sieve. Rise beans under cold running water. Discard any damaged beans. In a dutch oven cover beans with water. Cover and let stand in a cool place for 6 to 8 hours or overnight; drain. Rinse beans thoroughly under cold running water.

Return beans to the dutch oven. Add 6 cups fresh water. Add celery, prosciutto or Canadian bacon, garlic, oil, salt, and pepper. Bring to boiling; reduce heat.

Cover and simmer for 1½ to 2 hours or till beans are tender, stirring occasionally. Boil pasta in salted water until al dente. Drain and add to soup.

Makes 6 servings.

 ## Soaking Dry Beans

There are two easy ways to soak beans before cooking. For the first method, in a dutch oven bring beans and water to boiling. Reduce heat. Simmer, uncovered, for 2 minutes. Remove from heat. Cover and let stand for 1 hour. Drain and rinse beans.

For the second method, combine beans and cold water. Cover container. Let stand in a cool place for 6 to 8 hours or overnight. If the room is warm, soak beans in the refrigerator. Drain and rinse beans. Continue as directed in the recipes.

 # Potato and Leek Soup

4   leeks, sliced
½   cup butter or margarine
¼   cup flour
12 cups milk
1   teaspoon salt
½   teaspoon pepper
9   medium potatoes, peeled and cubed
½   cup chopped parsley
½   cup dry white wine

In a large saucepan cook leeks in butter or margarine till tender. Stir in flour. Add milk, salt, and pepper. Cook and stir till thickened and bubbly. Add potatoes.

Simmer, uncovered, about 1 hour or till potatoes are tender. Mash potatoes slightly, if desired. Stir in parsley and wine. Heat through (do not boil).

Makes 10 servings.

Clam Chowder

This is one of my staple recipes—I can almost make it with my eyes closed. I prepare it both at the store and at home.

3   stalks celery, sliced
1   medium onion, chopped
¼   cup olive oil
2   16-ounce cans tomatoes, cut up
4   medium potatoes, peeled and cubed
3   carrots, sliced
1   teaspoon dried parsley
1   teaspoon dried basil, crushed
1   teaspoon fines herbes
1   teaspoon salt
½   teaspoon pepper
2   7 ½-ounce cans minced clams

In a large saucepan cook celery and onion in oil till tender. Add tomatoes, potatoes, carrots, parsley, basil, fines herbes, salt, and pepper. Bring to boiling; reduce heat.

Cover and simmer for 30 minutes. Add minced clams. Simmer, uncovered, for 15 minutes more or till potatoes are tender.

Makes 4 to 6 servings.

 # Split Pea Soup

1   pound dry green split peas
8   cups water
5   carrots, sliced
5   stalks celery, sliced
1   medium onion, chopped
1   meaty ham bone or piece of prosciutto
½   teaspoon salt
½   teaspoon pepper
¼   teaspoon garlic powder

Place peas in a colander or sieve. Rinse under cold running water. In a dutch oven combine peas, 8 cups water, carrots, celery, onion, ham bone or prosciutto, salt, pepper, and garlic powder.

Bring split pea mixture to boiling; reduce heat. Cover and simmer for 1 hour. Remove ham bone; when cool enough to handle, cut off meat and coarsely chop. Discard bone. Return meat to soup.

Simmer for 30 minutes more. Mash peas slightly, if desired.

Makes 6 servings.

 ## Minestrone Soup

1	large onion, chopped
½	cup olive oil
12	cups water
2	16-ounce cans tomatoes, cut up
3	medium potatoes, peeled and chopped
1	bunch broccoli, cut into bite-size pieces
1	head cauliflower, cut into bite-size pieces
3	carrots, sliced
2	medium zucchini, sliced
1	pound fresh spinach, torn
1	17-ounce can whole kernel corn, drained
1	16-ounce can peas, drained
1	teaspoon salt
½	teaspoon pepper
¼	teaspoon garlic powder
¼	teaspoon dried tarragon, crushed
¼	teaspoon dried basil, crushed
1	cup grated Parmesan cheese

A great classic—perfect for cold weather.

In a large dutch oven cook onion in oil till tender. Add water, tomatoes, potatoes, broccoli, cauliflower, carrots, zucchini, spinach, corn, peas, salt, pepper, garlic powder, tarragon, and basil. Bring to boiling; reduce heat.

Simmer, uncovered, for 1 hour. Serve with grated Parmesan cheese.

Makes 12 servings.

Chicken and Tortellini Soup

We often turn to this soup when we are putting together a family menu.

1   2½- to 3-pound chicken, cut up
12   cups water
5   large carrots, sliced
1   medium onion, chopped
4   celery stalks, sliced
1   teaspoon salt
½   teaspoon pepper
½   teaspoon onion powder
½   teaspoon celery seed
    Dash garlic powder
1   pound beef tortellini

Rinse chicken; pat dry with paper towels. In a dutch oven combine water, chicken pieces, carrots, onion, celery, salt, pepper, onion powder, celery seed, and garlic powder. Bring to boiling; reduce heat.

Simmer, uncovered, for 1 hour. Add beef tortellini. Simmer about 15 minutes more or till tortellini is tender.

Makes 6 servings.

SALADS

Salads know no season. They are popular with our family and customers all year long. The most important thing to remember is that using the freshest ingredients can make the difference between an ordinary salad and a great one.

Among the favorite salad ingredients we always have on hand are Italian olive oils, Italian vinegars, anchovies, mustards, and grated cheeses. Of these, the two most important are the oil and vinegar. We like to use extra virgin olive oil and red or white wine vinegars for most of our salads. A light coating of oil and vinegar adds flavor but lets the taste of the other ingredients come through.

❧ Romaine and Blue Cheese Salad ❧

1 medium head Romaine lettuce, torn
2 medium tomatoes, cut into wedges
8 ounces blue cheese, crumbled
2 tablespoons olive oil
2 tablespoons red or white wine vinegar
  Salt
  Pepper

This is the perfect salad to serve with pasta. It's simple and delicious. We make a huge batch every day for the store.

In a salad bowl combine lettuce, tomatoes, and blue cheese. Stir together oil and vinegar. Pour over lettuce mixture, tossing to coat. Season with salt and pepper.

Makes 6 servings.

❧ Eggplant Salad (Caponata) ❧

4 medium eggplants
2 16-ounce cans tomatoes, cut up
20 Calamata olives, pitted, or pitted ripe olives
4 stalks celery, sliced
2 tablespoons olive oil
1 teaspoon sugar
½ teaspoon salt
½ teaspoon pepper
1 3 ½-ounce jar capers, drained
4 ounces pine nuts

We serve this great Sicilian salad every day in the store.

Wash eggplants and cut into cubes. In a shallow baking pan combine cubed eggplant, tomatoes, olives, celery, oil, sugar, salt, and pepper. Stir till well combined.

Bake eggplant mixture, uncovered, in a 375°F oven about 1 hour or till the vegetables are tender, stirring occasionally. Transfer to a bowl. Add capers and pine nuts. Cover and chill for several hours.

Makes 6 to 8 servings.

Mozzarella and Tomato Salad

1   pound mozzarella cheese, cut into
    bite-size pieces
1   large tomato, cut into wedges
2   stalks celery, sliced
1   small red onion, sliced
1   cucumber, peeled and sliced
¼   cup chopped parsley or fresh basil
2   tablespoons olive oil
2   tablespoons vinegar
1   teaspoon Dijon mustard
    Salt
    Pepper

In a large mixing bowl combine mozzarella cheese, tomato, celery, onion, cucumber, and parsley or basil. Stir together oil, vinegar, and mustard. Pour over cheese mixture, tossing to coat. Season with salt and pepper. Cover and chill for several hours.

Makes 4 servings.

Crab Salad

This is wonderful with fresh tomatoes, Italian olives, roasted peppers, and a big hunk of bread. And don't forget the chilled white wine!

1   pound fresh or frozen crabmeat
½   cup mayonnaise or salad dressing
3   stalks celery, finely chopped
1   small onion, chopped
2   carrots, finely chopped
8   pimiento-stuffed olives, sliced
2   pickled chili peppers, chopped
2   tablespoons chopped parsley
½   teaspoon salt
¼   teaspoon pepper

If using frozen crabmeat, thaw. Flake crabmeat into a mixing bowl. Stir in mayonnaise or salad dressing, celery, onion, carrots, olives, peppers, parsley, salt, and pepper.

Makes 4 to 6 servings.

Crab and Shrimp Salad

1   pound fresh or frozen crabmeat
12 ounces fresh or frozen shelled shrimp, cooked
12 Calamata olives, pitted, or pitted ripe olives
3   stalks celery, finely chopped
1   medium onion, chopped
2   tablespoons chopped parsley
2   tablespoons olive oil
2   tablespoons white wine vinegar
    Fresh ground pepper
    Lettuce leaves
    Cherry tomatoes
    Parsley sprigs

If using frozen crabmeat, thaw. Flake crabmeat into a mixing bowl. Stir in shrimp, olives, celery, onion, and parsley. Add oil and vinegar; toss to coat. Season with pepper.

Line 8 salad plates with leaf lettuce. Spoon crab and shrimp mixture on lettuce-lined plates. Garnish with tomatoes and parsley.

Makes 8 servings.

Tomato and Onion Salad

2   large tomatoes, cut into wedges
1   medium red onion, sliced
1   cup cold water
2   tablespoons olive oil
1   teaspoon dried oregano, crushed
    Salt
    Pepper

Serve this with hunks of crusty bread to sop up the dressing.

In a mixing bowl combine tomatoes, onion, water, oil, and oregano. Season with salt and pepper. Cover and chill for several hours.

Makes 4 servings.

Layered Mozzarella Salad

We use fresh, unsalted mozzarella cheese for this delectable salad. A loaf of crusty bread is the best accompaniment.

1   pound mozzarella cheese, sliced into 8 pieces
8   slices prosciutto or Canadian bacon
1   large tomato, cut into 8 slices
1   small red onion, cut into 8 slices
8   fresh basil leaves
    Fresh ground pepper
    Olive oil

On a serving tray layer mozzarella cheese, prosciutto or Canadian bacon, tomato, and onion. Top with basil; sprinkle with pepper. Drizzle lightly with oil.

Makes 8 servings.

Shrimp and Pasta Salad

I love this salad! Try it in the summer with fresh corn on the cob and warm bread.

8   ounces conchigliette (small shells)
4   cups water
1   teaspoon salt
1   pound fresh or frozen shelled shrimp
½   cup sliced green olives
1   large onion, chopped
3   stalks celery, sliced
2   carrots, chopped
⅓   cup mayonnaise or salad dressing
1   tablespoon white wine vinegar
1   tablespoon dill pickle juice
     Salt
     Pepper

Cook conchigliette in boiling water for 8 to 9 minutes or till al dente. Drain. Meanwhile, in a 3-quart saucepan bring the 4 cups water and 1 teaspoon salt to boiling. Add shrimp.

Return to boiling. Reduce heat. Simmer, uncovered, for 1 to 3 minutes or till shrimp turn pink; stir occasionally. Drain. Rinse shrimp under cold running water.

In a mixing bowl combine pasta, shrimp, olives, onion, celery, and carrots. Stir together mayonnaise or salad dressing, vinegar, and pickle juice. Stir into shrimp mixture. Season with salt and pepper. Cover and chill for several hours.

Makes 4 to 6 servings.

Chicken Salad

2   **cups finely chopped cooked chicken**
3   **stalks celery, chopped**
½   **cup seedless grapes, halved**
⅓   **cup raisins**
1   **7 ½-ounce can artichoke hearts, drained and sliced**
6   **pitted ripe olives, sliced**
½   **cup mayonnaise or salad dressing**
      Fresh ground pepper

This simple but elegant chicken salad is good with sliced avocado and toast.

In a mixing bowl combine chicken, celery, grapes, raisins, artichoke hearts, and olives. Stir in mayonnaise or salad dressing. Season with pepper.

Makes 4 servings.

Cooking Chicken

When a recipe calls for cooked chicken and you don't have any leftovers, follow these directions for cooking raw chicken breasts.

For 2 cups cooked, diced chicken, use 2 whole medium chicken breasts, halved lengthwise, or ¾ pound skinned and boned chicken breasts. In a 10-inch skillet bring 1⅓ cups water to boiling. Add chicken breasts. Cover and simmer for 18 to 20 minutes for whole breasts, or 12 to 14 minutes for boneless pieces, or till done.

Marinated Mushrooms

We never get a chance to marinate these for long because they sell so fast at our store.

3 medium green or red sweet peppers, sliced
4 cloves garlic, finely chopped
½ cup olive oil
1 pound fresh mushrooms
3 tablespoons lemon juice
½ teaspoon salt
   Dash pepper

Place peppers and garlic in a shallow baking pan. Toss with oil. Bake in a 375°F oven about 15 minutes or till tender. Cool.

Meanwhile, remove and discard mushroom stems. Boil mushroom caps in water for 2 minutes; drain. In a mixing bowl combine mushrooms, pepper mixture, lemon juice, salt, and pepper. Toss to combine. Cover and chill for several hours.

Makes 4 servings.

Grandma's
Marinated Mushrooms

My sister Linda would kill for these mushrooms! Grandma fixes them for all of our family gatherings.

1 pound fresh mushrooms
1 cup vinegar
1 cup olive oil
4 cloves garlic, finely chopped
   Dash ground red pepper
   Dash salt

Remove and discard mushroom stems. Halve any large mushrooms. In a saucepan bring vinegar to boiling. Add mushrooms and boil for 1 minute. Drain.

In a mixing bowl combine the mushrooms, oil, garlic, red pepper, and salt. Toss to combine. Cover and chill for several hours.

Makes 4 servings.

Mushrooms

Here's a rundown of different types of mushrooms available fresh and sometimes dried.

&• Chanterelles are sometimes called "little goblets" because they are shaped like cups. They are reddish yellow and have a mild apricot taste.

&• Morels have a woodsy flavor similar to truffles. Look for them at specialty food shops.

&• Porcini mushrooms, also called "little pigs," come from Italy. They have a rich flavor that goes well with game and poultry.

Roman Three-Bean Salad

1	16-ounce can garbanzo beans, drained
1	16-ounce can small white beans, drained
1	16-ounce can red roman or kidney beans, drained
3	stalks celery, sliced
1	medium onion, chopped
¼	cup chopped parsley
⅓	cup vinegar
¼	cup olive oil
1	tablespoon Dijon mustard
	Pinch of dried tarragon, crushed
	Salt
	Pepper

This is a good party salad. You can easily double it to serve a crowd of hungry friends and family.

In a large mixing bowl combine garbanzo beans, white beans, red or kidney beans, celery, onion, and parsley. Stir together vinegar, oil, mustard, and tarragon. Pour over bean mixture. Toss to coat. Season with salt and pepper. Cover and chill for several hours.

Makes 8 servings.

Marinated Artichoke Salad

This is fantastic served with prosciutto wrapped around breadsticks.

2   14-ounce cans artichoke hearts, drained
½   cup olive oil
1   teaspoon salt
½   teaspoon dried oregano, crushed

Cut artichoke hearts into bite-size pieces. In a mixing bowl combine artichoke hearts, oil, salt, and oregano. Stir till well combined. Serve at room temperature.

Makes 4 servings.

Sun-Dried Tomatoes

Look for sun-dried tomatoes in the produce section of your local supermarket, at an Italian food shop, or at a specialty food store.

1   pound sun-dried tomatoes
1   3 ½-ounce jar capers, drained
3   cloves garlic, finely chopped
    Olive oil

Place sun-dried tomatoes in a saucepan. Cover with water. Bring to boiling. Cover and continue boiling for 3 to 4 minutes or till tender. Drain.

Transfer tomatoes to 3 or 4 clean pint jars. Divide capers and garlic among the jars, mix well, and cover mixture with oil. Seal jars tightly with lids. Store in the refrigerator.

Sun-Dried Tomato and Ricotta Salad

If you can't find fresh, solid ricotta cheese, you can use mozzarella, edam, or gouda instead.

1   pound ricotta cheese
2   pint jars Sun-Dried Tomatoes (see recipe, above)

Cut ricotta into bite-size pieces. In a mixing bowl combine ricotta and sun-dried tomatoes. Stir till well combined.

Makes 8 servings.

Tripe Salad

2 to 3 pounds beef tripe
4 cloves garlic, finely chopped
¼ cup chopped parsley
2 tablespoons olive oil
2 tablespoons vinegar
3 tablespoons lemon juice
Salt
Pepper

Serve this main dish salad with fresh sliced tomatoes and whole grain bread.

Place tripe in a large saucepan; cover with water and boil about 50 minutes or till tender. Drain. When tripe is cool enough to handle, trim off excess fat and cut tripe into bite-size pieces.

In a mixing bowl combine cooked tripe, garlic, parsley, oil, vinegar, and lemon juice. Season with salt and pepper. Cover and chill for several hours.

Makes 8 to 10 servings.

Antipasto

4 ounces large black pepper olives or pitted ripe olives
1 6-ounce jar marinated artichoke hearts, drained
8 ounces unsalted mozzarella cheese, sliced
8 ounces smoked mozzarella, sliced
4 ounces prosciutto or Canadian bacon, sliced
4 ounces dried Italian sausage, sliced

We eat this as a salad course, but it can also serve as a delicious appetizer.

In the center of a serving platter arrange olives and artichoke hearts. Place unsalted mozzarella cheese, smoked mozzarella cheese, prosciutto or Canadian bacon, and Italian sausage around olives and artichokes.

Makes 4 servings.

Fresh Green Bean Salad

Serve with grilled hamburgers and fried potatoes.

1   pound fresh green beans, trimmed
2   medium tomatoes, cut into wedges
1   medium onion, sliced
¼   cup olive oil
¼   cup red wine vinegar

Boil beans in water for 20 to 25 minutes or till crisp-tender. Drain. In a mixing bowl combine beans, tomatoes, and onion. Toss with oil and vinegar. Cover and chill for several hours.

Makes 4 servings.

 # Radicchio Salad

For a beautiful presentation, serve this salad in a white or black ceramic bowl. It tastes great with a large piece of blue cheese, brick-oven bread, and sweet butter.

4   small heads radicchio, torn
2   medium tomatoes, sliced
1   medium red onion, sliced
¼   cup chopped fresh basil or parsley
2   tablespoons olive oil
2   tablespoons vinegar
    Salt
    Pepper

In a large mixing bowl combine radicchio, tomatoes, onion, and basil or parsley. Toss with oil and vinegar. Season with salt and pepper. Cover and chill for several hours.

Makes 4 servings.

 ## Radicchio

Radicchio is also called Italian lettuce, and radicchio is the Italian term for all chicories. Red radicchio is red Verona chicory. It grows in small, round heads with thick, red leaves and white veins. Its flavor is refreshingly bitter, so radicchio is best when mixed with milder tasting greens. It holds up well to a hearty oil and vinegar dressing.

Radicchio and Fennel Salad

4   small heads radicchio, torn
2   medium cucumbers, peeled and sliced
1   medium fennel, sliced
1   small onion, sliced
¼   cup chopped parsley
⅓   cup olive oil
¼   cup balsamic vinegar
    Salt
    Pepper

I love this with Genoa tuna and toast.

In a mixing bowl combine radicchio, cucumbers, fennel, onion, and parsley. Toss with oil and vinegar. Season with salt and pepper.

Makes 4 servings.

Tortellini Salad

6   cups water
1   pound tortellini
1   bunch broccoli, cut into bite-size pieces
2   cups cherry tomatoes
¼   cup chopped parsley
2   tablespoons olive oil
2   tablespoons balsamic vinegar
    Salt
    Pepper

In a large saucepan bring water to boiling. Add tortellini. Return to boiling; reduce heat. Cover and simmer for 5 minutes. Add broccoli. Cover and simmer for 5 to 7 minutes more or till tortellini and broccoli are tender. Drain and cool.

In a mixing bowl combine tortellini, broccoli, tomatoes, and parsley. Toss with oil and vinegar. Season with salt and pepper. Cover and chill for several hours.

Makes 8 servings.

Scungilli Salad

We prepare this salad on Christmas Eve, adhering to the Italian tradition of eating only fish on this day.

3   8-ounce cans scungilli (conch)
12 Calamata olives, pitted, or pitted ripe olives
3   stalks celery, sliced
1   medium onion, chopped
1   cup chopped parsley
½   cup vinegar peppers, sliced
1   clove garlic, finely chopped
2   tablespoons olive oil
2   tablespoons red wine vinegar
    Salt
    Pepper

Drain scungilli, reserving liquid. In a large mixing bowl combine scungilli, olives, celery, onion, parsley, peppers, and garlic. Toss with oil, vinegar, and reserved liquid. Season with salt and pepper. Cover and chill for several hours.

Makes 6 to 8 servings.

 ## Octopus Salad

This is one of my father's favorite salads. He could eat the whole batch himself! A glass of chardonnay and seeded Italian bread are the perfect accompaniments.

3   pounds fresh octopus, cleaned
10 Calamata olives, pitted, or pitted ripe olives
2   stalks celery, sliced
2   medium green or red sweet peppers, chopped
¼   cup chopped parsley
4   cloves garlic, finely chopped
2   tablespoons olive oil
2   tablespoons red wine vinegar
1   tablespoon lemon juice
    Salt
    Pepper

Place octopus in a Dutch oven; cover with water. Bring to a boil and cook the octopus for 25 to 30 minutes or till tender. Drain, rinse, and remove skin. Cut octopus into bite-size pieces.

In a large mixing bowl stir together octopus, olives, celery, peppers, parsley, and garlic. Toss with oil, vinegar, and lemon juice. Season with salt and pepper. Cover and chill for several hours.

Makes 6 servings.

 ## Fresh Beet Salad

4	medium fresh beets (about 1 ¼ pounds)
1	large onion, sliced
¼	cup olive oil
¼	cup red wine vinegar
	Salt
	Pepper

Save the greens from the fresh beets and use them to make the Warm Beet Greens Salad, below.

Wash and peel beets. Boil whole beets in water for 20 minutes or till tender. Drain. Cut into ¼-inch slices. In a mixing bowl combine beets and onion. Toss with oil and vinegar. Season with salt and pepper. Cover and chill for several hours.

Makes 4 servings.

 ## Warm Beet Greens Salad

	Beet greens from 4 medium fresh beets
2	cups water
2	tablespoons olive oil
	Salt
	Pepper

This simple salad can also be served as a vegetable side dish.

Wash beet greens. In a saucepan combine beet greens and water. Bring to boiling; reduce heat. Cover and simmer for 5 to 7 minutes or till tender. Drain.

Place cooked beet greens in a mixing bowl. Add oil, tossing to coat greens. Season with salt and pepper.

Makes 4 servings.

Arugula Salad

There is no vinegar in this salad, so make sure you use a good quality extra virgin olive oil.

1   large bunch arugula
2   large tomatoes, diced
1   red onion, thinly sliced
¼ to ⅓ cup olive oil
     Salt
     Pepper

Cut stems off arugula and discard. Rinse arugula leaves well under running water. Pat dry with paper towels. Cut arugula leaves in half. In a large bowl combine arugula, tomatoes, onion, and olive oil. Toss well. Season with salt and pepper.

Makes 4 to 6 servings.

Arugula and Yellow Pepper Salad

Serve this with Italian dried sausages, brick-oven bread, and provolone cheese.

2   heads arugula, torn
3   medium yellow sweet peppers, sliced
1   cup cherry tomatoes
⅓   cup broken walnuts
⅓   cup seedless white raisins
¼   cup white wine vinegar
2   tablespoons olive oil
2   tablespoons mayonnaise or salad dressing
1   teaspoon salt
½   teaspoon sugar
     Fresh ground pepper

In a mixing bowl combine arugula, peppers, tomatoes, walnuts, and raisins. Stir together vinegar, oil, mayonnaise or salad dressing, salt, sugar, and pepper. Pour over arugula mixture, tossing to coat. Serve immediately or cover and chill for several hours.

Makes 4 servings.

Romaine Salad

1   medium head romaine lettuce, torn
2   medium tomatoes, cut into wedges
1   small red onion, sliced
4   ounces blue cheese, crumbled
5   anchovy fillets
¾   cup olive oil
     Juice of 2 lemons
     Anchovy fillets (optional)

The secret to this flavorful salad is anchovies. Even if you don't like anchovies, you'll like the way they taste in the dressing.

In a large mixing bowl combine romaine, tomatoes, onion, and cheese.

For salad dressing, in a small bowl mash anchovies. Stir in olive oil and lemon juice till well combined. Pour over romaine mixture and toss to coat. Serve immediately. Garnish each serving with anchovy fillets, if desired.

Makes 4 servings.

 # Salad Amalfi

1   9 ¼-ounce can tuna, drained and flaked
8   ounces mozzarella cheese, sliced
4   ounces salami, sliced
1   small tomato, cut into wedges
4   slices red onion
12   Calamata olives, pitted, or pitted ripe olives
     Fresh lemon juice
     Lemon slices (optional)

We ate this when we were in Italy in a little town called Positano on the Amalfi coast. Serve it as we had it there—with chilled white wine.

Arrange tuna in the center of a serving platter. Surround tuna with cheese, salami, tomato, onion, and olives. Squeeze lemon juice over tuna. Garnish platter with lemon slices, if desired.

Makes 4 servings.

Cucumber Salad

Our next door neighbor, Frances, made this for us many times as we were growing up. She always used fresh cucumbers from her garden and served the salad with breaded veal cutlets and buttered rye bread.

2 large cucumbers, peeled and thinly sliced
2 tablespoons olive oil
2 tablespoons red wine vinegar
½ teaspoon sugar
   Salt
   Pepper

In a mixing bowl stir together cucumbers, oil, vinegar, and sugar. Season with salt and pepper. Cover and chill for several hours.

Makes 4 servings.

 # Finocchi (Fennel) Salad

You can simplify this salad by using only the fennel with oil, vinegar, salt, and pepper.

2 medium fennel, sliced
2 medium tomatoes, cut into wedges
12 pitted Sicilian green olives
2 cloves garlic, finely chopped
2 tablespoons olive oil
2 tablespoons vinegar
   Salt
   Pepper
½ pound Parmesan cheese, crumbled into small pieces

In a mixing bowl combine fennel, tomatoes, olives, and garlic. Toss with oil and vinegar. Season with salt and pepper. Sprinkle with Parmesan cheese.

Makes 4 servings.

Christmas Fruit

2   red prickly pears
4   kiwi fruit

Peel prickly pears and kiwi fruit. Slice each fruit into 1/4 inch slices. On salad plates, alternate slices of prickly pear and kiwi.

Makes 4 servings.

Prickly Pears

One of the newest, most exciting fruits to arrive on the produce scene is the prickly pear. This unique fruit of the Nopal cactus plant thrives in the Mediterranean, Australia, Mexico, and Southern California. The prickly pear is actually a large berry with small edible seeds similar to raspberry seeds. Some compare the taste to that of fresh, ripe watermelon. To peel, cut a small section off the tip of the fruit, make three slits from the tip to the stem, and lift off the skin. Prickly pears are generally available year-round and should be used within three days to one week for best flavor.

SAUCES

auces are among the easiest Italian specialties to prepare; the key to success is patience. Most of our sauces should be slowly simmered till all the flavors blend together. The best way to determine whether a sauce is done is to look at it. When the oil used in cooking rises to the top and separates into thin streams, the sauce is ready.

We serve most of the recipes in this chapter with one pound of pasta. Our rule of thumb is to pair hearty, robust sauces with more durable pastas such as rigatoni or mostaccioli. Delicate white sauces are better suited for fine pastas such as capellini or vermicelli. But the bottom line is that all of these flavorful sauces can be matched with any pasta of your choice.

Meat Sauce

1 ½ pounds ground beef
1   pound link sausage, sliced
1   medium onion, chopped
2   tablespoons olive oil
4   16-ounce cans tomatoes
½   cup dry white wine
    Salt
    Pepper
    Garlic powder
    Oregano

This sauce and Marinara Sauce are the staple of many of our recipes. The flavor of Meat Sauce will vary depending on the type of the sausage you use.

In a large saucepan cook ground beef, sausage, and onion in oil till meat is brown. Stir in tomatoes and wine. Season with salt, pepper, garlic powder, and oregano. Bring to boiling; reduce heat.

Simmer, uncovered, for 45 to 60 minutes, stirring occasionally.

Makes about 8 cups sauce.

Marinara Sauce

7   cloves garlic, finely chopped
2   tablespoons olive oil
4   16-ounce cans tomatoes, cut up
    Salt
    Pepper
    Oregano

This sauce is so versatile! It's great on plain pasta or as an ingredient in other recipes throughout this book.

In a large saucepan cook garlic in oil till tender but not brown. Add tomatoes, mash slightly. Season with salt, pepper, and oregano. Bring to boiling; reduce heat.

Simmer, uncovered, for 30 minutes.

Makes about 6 cups sauce.

Tuna-Tomato Sauce

Delicious! I never liked canned tuna until I came up with this recipe, which I like to serve with 1 pound of cooked penne.

1   **medium onion, chopped**
2   **tablespoons olive oil**
2   **16-ounce cans tomatoes, cut up**
1   **12½-ounce can tuna, drained and flaked**
1   **16-ounce can peas, drained**
     Salt
     Pepper
     Oregano
½   **cup grated Romano cheese**

In a large skillet cook onion in oil till tender. Add tomatoes, tuna, and peas. Season with salt, pepper, and a dash of oregano. Bring to boiling; reduce heat. Simmer, uncovered, for 25 minutes. Serve with grated cheese.

Makes about 8 cups sauce.

 # Red Clam Sauce

6   **cloves garlic, finely chopped**
2   **tablespoons olive oil**
2   **7½-ounce cans minced clams**
1   **16-ounce can tomatoes, cut up**
     Salt
     Pepper
⅓   **cup chopped parsley**

In a saucepan cook garlic in oil till tender but not brown. Add undrained clams and tomatoes. Season with salt and pepper. Bring to boiling; reduce heat. Simmer, uncovered, for 15 minutes. Sprinkle with parsley.

Makes about 3 cups sauce.

White Clam Sauce

6   cloves garlic, finely chopped
½   cup olive oil
2   7½-ounce cans minced clams
    Salt
    Pepper
⅓   cup chopped parsley

This is a classic Italian sauce that our family has enjoyed for years.

In a saucepan cook garlic in oil till tender but not brown. Add undrained clams. Season with salt and pepper. Bring to boiling; reduce heat.

Simmer, uncovered, for 10 minutes. Sprinkle with parsley. Makes about 2 cups sauce. To use fresh clams, substitute 36 little neck clams for the 2 cans minced clams.

 Salsa di Napoli

1   large onion, sliced
¼   cup olive oil
4   16-ounce cans tomatoes, cut up
4   large or 6 small potatoes, peeled and cubed
½   cup fresh basil, chopped
    Salt
    Pepper
1   cup grated Parmesan cheese

This recipe is very starchy but totally delicious. It comes from the Amalfi coast of Italy. We serve it with 1 pound of cooked rigatoni and sprinkle on 1 cup grated cheese.

In a large saucepan cook onion in oil till tender. Add tomatoes, potatoes, and basil. Season with salt and pepper. Bring to boiling; reduce heat.

Simmer, uncovered, for 1½ hours. Stir in Parmesan cheese. Cook for 5 minutes more.

Makes about 10 cups sauce.

62

 ## Pesto

This sauce is my pride and joy. It's different from most pesto sauces because it's cooked briefly to bring out the flavors. I call it peasant-style pesto because the ingredients are finely chopped instead of pureed in a blender or food processor. The recipe makes enough for 3 pounds of pasta. If it's too much for you to use at once, you can store it in the freezer for several months (without cheese).

10	cloves garlic, finely chopped
2	cups olive oil
6	cups finely chopped fresh basil
½	cup pine nuts or walnuts, finely chopped
1	teaspoon salt
1	teaspoon pepper
2	cups grated Romano cheese

In a large skillet cook garlic in oil till tender. Add basil and nuts. Cook and stir over medium heat for 5 minutes. Season with salt and pepper. Stir in cheese just before serving.

Makes 3 to 4 cups sauce.

 ## Carbonaro Sauce

Made with ricotta cheese, our recipe is lighter than most classic Carbonaro sauces.

12	ounces pancetta or Canadian bacon, diced
1	small onion, chopped
¼	cup butter or margarine
1½	cups ricotta cheese
1	16-ounce can peas, drained
½	cup grated Parmesan cheese
	Salt
	Pepper

In a medium skillet cook pancetta or Canadian bacon and onion in butter till onion is tender. Stir in ricotta, peas, and Parmesan cheese. Season with salt and pepper. Cook and stir over low heat till mixture is creamy and heated through.

Makes about 4 cups sauce.

Sausage and Basil Sauce

1   pound Italian sausage
1   medium onion, sliced
2   16-ounce cans tomatoes, cut up
    Salt
    Pepper
    Garlic powder
½   cup chopped fresh basil

This summer sauce is out of this world! Serve it with 1 pound of gnocchi or rigatoni.

In a large skillet cook sausage and onion in oil till sausage is brown. Add tomatoes. Bring to boiling; reduce heat. Simmer, uncovered, for 35 to 40 minutes or till desired consistency. Season with salt, pepper, and garlic powder. Stir in basil.

Makes about 4 cups sauce.

Zucchini and Tomato Sauce

1   medium onion, sliced
2   tablespoons olive oil
4 or 5   medium zucchini, cut into julienne strips
2   16-ounce cans tomatoes, cut up
         Salt
         Pepper
         Garlic powder

We typically serve this fresh-tasting sauce with 1 pound of macaroni.

In a large saucepan cook onion in oil till tender. Add zucchini and cook till lightly browned. Add tomatoes. Season with salt, pepper, and garlic powder. Bring to boiling; reduce heat. Simmer, uncovered, for 30 to 40 minutes or till desired consistency.

Makes about 4 cups sauce.

64

Putanesca Sauce

Another fabulous summer sauce! This is known as the "whore sauce of Naples."

4	cloves garlic, finely chopped
2	tablespoons olive oil
15	Calamata olives, pitted, or pitted ripe olives
2	16-ounce cans tomatoes
½	of a 2-ounce can anchovy fillets, mashed
1	3-ounce bottle (¼ cup) capers in brine
⅓	cup chopped parsley
	Salt
	Pepper

In a large skillet cook garlic in oil till tender but not brown. Add olives, tomatoes, anchovies, capers, and parsley. Season with salt and pepper. Bring mixture to boiling; reduce heat. Simmer, uncovered, for 45 minutes.

Makes about 4 cups sauce.

Manganaro's
White Cream Sauce

Serve this by tossing it with 1 pound of cooked fettuccine. Transfer to a serving platter and sprinkle with 1 cup grated Parmesan cheese.

½	cup butter or margarine
½	cup milk
2	cups ricotta cheese
	Salt
	Pepper

In a medium saucepan melt butter or margarine. Stir in milk. Add ricotta and stir till well combined. Season with salt and pepper. Cook and stir over low heat till heated through.

Makes about 3 cups sauce.

PASTA

A hhh . . . pasta. We love it! When we were growing up we ate pasta every single night, in every shape, form, and flavor, and never got tired of it. Needless to say, we were chubby kids. Then we moved to New Jersey and realized the rest of the world was thin, so we started eating like other people. But, to this day, we are a pasta-loving family. We still enjoy such childhood favorites as Filetto di Pomodori and Rotelle with Eggplant and Sausage, and we think you will enjoy them too.

Lasagna

4	**cups Meat Sauce**
4	**meatballs (optional)**
1	**pound link sausage, sliced**
1	**pound lasagna noodles**
1	**pound ricotta cheese**
2	**eggs**
1	**pound mozzarella cheese, sliced**
1	**cup grated Parmesan cheese**

This is one of the most popular dishes at our store. Our customers tell us there is no other lasagna like it.

Prepare Meat Sauce. If desired, prepare Marion's Meatballs; mash cooked meatballs with a fork. Set aside. Place uncooked sausages in an unheated skillet. Add 1/2 cup water. Cover and cook slowly for 5 minutes; drain. Uncover and cook slowly for 12 to 14 minutes or till liquid from sausages has evaporated and sausages are done.

Meanwhile, in a large kettle cook lasagna noodles in boiling water for 8 to 9 minutes or till almost al dente. Drain. In a mixing bowl stir together ricotta cheese and eggs.

To assemble, layer bottom of a 13 × 9 × 2-inch pan with lasagna noodles. Spread with one-third of the ricotta mixture. Sprinkle one-third of the sausage and meatball mixture over ricotta mixture. Dot with some of the meat sauce. Layer one-third of the mozzarella over meat sauce. Sprinkle with one-third of the Parmesan. Repeat layers, ending with mozzarella. Dot with sauce (save about 2 cups sauce to serve with lasagna).

Bake, uncovered, in a 375°F oven for 30 to 40 minutes or till heated through. (Or assemble in advance and refrigerate, then bake 45 minutes.) Serve with remaining Meat Sauce and grated Parmesan.

Makes 8 servings.

Lasagna Primavera: Prepare Lasagna as directed, substituting 4 cups cooked vegetables for the sausage and meatballs. Use 4 cups Marinara Sauce or tomato sauce instead of Meat Sauce. Continue as directed.

Spaghetti Venezia

I had this recipe in Venice during one of the most romantic dinners of my life. Since then, I have made it many times at home.

1 medium onion, sliced
1 2-ounce can anchovy fillets
12 Calamata olives, pitted, or pitted ripe olives
2 tablespoons olive oil
  Pepper
1 pound whole wheat spaghetti
1 cup grated Romano cheese

In a large skillet cook onion, anchovies, and olives in oil till onion is tender. Mash anchovies with a fork. Season with pepper.

Meanwhile, cook pasta in boiling water for 10 to 12 minutes or till al dente. Drain. In a large bowl toss together cooked pasta and onion-anchovy mixture. Sprinkle with grated Romano cheese.

Makes 4 servings.

Baked Ziti with Eggplant

This is our Friday special at the store, and our customers love it. It's a wonderful meatless meal.

4 medium eggplants, peeled and cut crosswise into 20 slices (5 slices per eggplant)
2 to 3 cups flour
4 eggs
½ cup milk
¼ cup grated Parmesan cheese
1 cup olive oil
1 pound ziti (long tubular macaroni)
4 cups Marinara Sauce
2 ounces ricotta cheese
12 ounces mozzarella cheese, cut into cubes
½ cup grated Romano cheese

Coat eggplant slices with flour. Stir together eggs, milk, and Parmesan cheese. Dip floured eggplant into egg mixture. In a large skillet fry eggplant in a single layer in hot oil about 3 minutes per side or till brown. Drain on paper towels. Add more oil if necessary during frying.

Meanwhile, cook ziti in boiling water for 14 to 15 minutes or till al dente. Drain. Stir in 1 cup Marinara Sauce. Add ricotta and mozzarella cheese. Stir to combine.

Spread about one-third of the pasta mixture in the bottom of a 13 × 9 × 2-inch baking dish. Top with half of the fried eggplant. Repeat layers of pasta, eggplant, and pasta. Spread about 1 cup Marinara Sauce over the top. Bake, uncovered, in a 350°F oven for 40 minutes or till heated through. Meanwhile, heat remaining sauce in a saucepan. Serve sauce and Romano cheese with pasta mixture.

Makes 6 servings.

Baked Ziti: Prepare Baked Ziti with Eggplant as directed, omitting eggplant, flour, eggs, milk, Parmesan cheese, and olive oil.

Rotelle
with Eggplant and Sausage

1	**pound fennel sausage**
1	**medium onion, sliced**
2	**tablespoons olive oil**
3	**small eggplants, peeled and cubed**
	Salt
	Pepper
	Garlic powder
¼	**cup chopped parsley**
1	**pound rotelle (corkscrew or spiral macaroni)**
½	**cup grated Romano cheese**

Serve this during the summer with a hearty red wine and a simple tossed salad.

In a large skillet cook sausage and onion in oil till sausage is lightly brown. Stir in eggplant. Continue cooking for 10 to 15 minutes or till eggplant is tender. Season with salt, pepper, and garlic powder. Stir in parsley.

Meanwhile, cook rotelle in boiling water for 8 to 10 minutes or till al dente. Drain. In a large bowl toss together cooked rotelle and sausage-eggplant mixture. Sprinkle with grated Romano cheese.

Makes 4 to 6 servings.

Spaghetti with Eggplant

This simple recipe from Grandma D'Angelo is one of our family favorites.

4   cloves garlic, finely chopped
¼   cup olive oil
4   small eggplants, thinly sliced
1   pound spaghetti
1   pound ricotta cheese
    Salt
    Pepper
½   cup grated Romano cheese

In a medium skillet cook garlic in oil till tender but not brown; remove garlic from oil. Add eggplant slices to skillet in a single layer. Cook eggplant in hot oil about 2 minutes per side or till golden brown. Remove eggplant from skillet; drain on paper towels. Repeat with remaining eggplant slices. Add more oil, if necessary, during cooking.

Meanwhile, cook spaghetti in boiling water for 10 to 12 minutes or till al dente. Drain. In a large bowl toss together cooked spaghetti, eggplant slices, and ricotta cheese. Season with salt and pepper. Sprinkle with grated Romano cheese.

Makes 4 to 6 servings.

 ## Eggplant

Eggplant has a subtle flavor which allows it to blend readily with other foods. Look for eggplant that has shiny, purple skin and firm flesh. Once you purchase eggplant, you can store it at room temperature for 1 to 2 days.

Sometimes eggplant has a bitter flavor. To eliminate this problem, cut eggplant as directed in the recipes and layer it in a colander, salting each layer. Let eggplant stand in colander about 1 hour to drain. Rinse and pat dry with paper towels. Continue as directed in the recipe.

Baked Fettuccine

1	pound spinach fettuccine
1	pound white fettuccine
1	large onion, sliced
1	stalk celery, finely chopped
¼	cup pine nuts
1	head garlic (15 to 20 cloves), finely chopped
1	cup olive oil
12	eggs
2	pounds unsalted mozzarella cheese, cubed
1	pound ham, cut into strips
2 ½	cups ricotta cheese
1 ½	cups grated Parmesan cheese
1	cup milk
1	tablespoon pepper
2	teaspoons salt
1	teaspoon dried basil
3	tablespoons butter or margarine
¼	cup dry bread crumbs

My sister Linda created this recipe for a special occasion, and it was a big hit. It's a good party dish because you can prepare it ahead of time and put it in the oven after your guests arrive.

In a dutch oven cook fettuccine in boiling water for 7 to 9 minutes or till almost al dente. Drain and set aside. Rinse to prevent sticking.

Meanwhile, in a large skillet cook onion, celery, pine nuts, and garlic in hot oil till onion is tender and nuts are brown. In a large bowl stir together eggs, mozzarella cheese, ham, ricotta cheese, Parmesan cheese, milk, pepper, salt, and basil. Stir in cooked pasta and onion mixture. Toss till well combined.

Generously butter the bottom and sides of a dutch oven. Sprinkle with bread crumbs. Transfer fettuccine mixture to dutch oven. Bake, uncovered, in a 300°F oven for 1 hour. Remove from oven and let stand for 20 minutes.

Use a spatula to loosen the pasta from the sides of the dutch oven. Place a large serving platter on top of the dutch oven. Invert the platter and dutch oven and unmold the pasta mixture onto the serving platter.

Makes 20 servings.

Filetto di Pomodori

This easy tomato-prosciutto pasta is one of my father's favorite dishes. He likes it with perciatelli (long, hollow, tubular pasta).

1	medium onion, sliced
2	cloves garlic, finely chopped
¼	cup butter or margarine
2	tablespoons olive oil
6	ounces diced prosciutto, pancetta, or Canadian bacon
1	16-ounce can tomatoes, cut up
	Salt
	Pepper
1	pound desired pasta
½	cup grated Parmesan or Romano cheese

In a large skillet cook onion and garlic in butter or margarine and oil till onion is tender. Add prosciutto, pancetta, or Canadian bacon. Cook and stir for 2 minutes. Add tomatoes. Bring to boiling; reduce heat. Simmer, uncovered, for 35 to 40 minutes or till desired consistency. Season with salt and pepper.

Meanwhile, cook pasta in boiling water till al dente. Drain. In a large bowl toss together cooked pasta and grated Parmesan or Romano cheese. Add tomato mixture. Sprinkle with additional grated Parmesan or Romano cheese, if desired.

Makes 4 servings.

Broccoli Capellini

We like to use angel hair pasta in this recipe, but you can use vermicelli or spaghettini instead.

6	cups water
1	bunch broccoli, cut into bite-size pieces
1	pound capellini (angel hair pasta)
1	medium onion, finely chopped
½	cup olive oil
	Salt
	Pepper
½	cup grated Romano cheese

In a large kettle or saucepan bring water to boiling. Add broccoli. Return to boiling; reduce heat. Cover and simmer for 5 to 6 minutes or till broccoli is crisp-tender. Remove broccoli and add pasta. Cook till al dente. Drain, reserving 1 cup cooking liquid.

Meanwhile, in a small skillet cook onion in oil till tender. In a large bowl toss together capellini and broccoli mixture, reserved cooking liquid, and onion mixture. (Mixture will be slightly soupy.) Season with salt and pepper. Sprinkle with grated Romano cheese.

Makes 4 to 6 servings.

 ## Macaroni Primavera

2	**medium potatoes, peeled and sliced**
1	**bunch broccoli, cut into bite-size pieces**
2	**medium carrots, sliced**
1	**medium onion, sliced**
½	**cup olive oil**
2	**medium zucchini, sliced**
8	**ounces fresh mushrooms, sliced**
	Salt
	Pepper
⅓	**cup chopped parsley**
1	**pound elbow macaroni**
	Dash of white wine (optional)
½	**cup grated Pepato cheese**

We add pizzazz to this pasta by sprinkling it with ½ cup Pepato cheese (Romano cheese with black peppercorns).

In a saucepan cook potatoes, broccoli, and carrots in boiling water for 10 minutes or till just crisp-tender. Drain. In a large skillet, cook onion in oil till onion is tender. Add potatoes, broccoli, carrots, zucchini, and mushrooms. Cook and stir over medium-high heat about 5 minutes or till vegetables are just tender. Season with salt and pepper. Stir in parsley.

Meanwhile, cook macaroni in boiling water for 10 minutes or till al dente. Drain. In a large bowl toss together cooked macaroni, wine (if desired), and vegetable mixture. Sprinkle with grated Pepato cheese.

Makes 4 to 6 servings.

Shrimp and Broccoli Conchiglie

We love this seafood dish with fresh sliced tomatoes, onion salad, and homemade bread.

1	**bunch broccoli, cut into bite-size pieces**
6	**cloves garlic, finely chopped**
½	**cup olive oil**
1	**pound fresh or frozen peeled and deveined shrimp**
⅓	**cup chopped fresh basil or parsley**
1	**pound conchiglie (medium shells)**
	Salt
	Pepper
½	**cup grated Pepato cheese**

In a saucepan cook broccoli in boiling water for 5 to 10 minutes or till crisp-tender. Drain; set aside.

In a large skillet cook garlic in oil till tender but not brown. Add shrimp and cook for 3 to 4 minutes more or till shrimp turn pink. Stir in broccoli and basil or parsley; heat through.

Meanwhile, cook conchiglie in boiling water for 12 to 14 minutes or till al dente. Drain. In a large bowl toss together cooked conchiglie and shrimp-broccoli mixture. Season with salt and pepper. Sprinkle with Pepato cheese.

Makes 4 to 6 servings.

Crab Capellini

Capellini cooks very fast compared to other pasta. Once it is tossed, it absorbs the sauce quickly.

8	**cloves garlic, finely chopped**
¾	**cup olive oil**
4	**16-ounce cans tomatoes, cut up**
8	**hard-shell blue crabs, live**
1	**pound capellini (angel hair pasta)**
1	**cup grated Parmesan cheese**

In a dutch oven cook garlic in oil till tender. Add tomatoes. Bring to boiling; reduce heat. Simmer, uncovered, for 15 minutes. Add crabs, one at a time, to tomato mixture. Cover and simmer for 20 minutes.

Meanwhile, cook pasta in boiling water for 5 to 6 minutes or till al dente. Drain. In a large bowl toss together pasta and crab mixture and arrange crabs on top. Sprinkle with Parmesan cheese.

Makes 4 servings.

 ## Seafood Linguine

4	quarts cold water
2	teaspoons salt
24	little neck clams in shells
6	cloves garlic, finely chopped
½	cup olive oil
1	32-ounce can tomatoes, cut up
1	pound fresh calamari, cleaned and cut up
⅓	cup chopped parsley
⅓	cup chopped fresh basil
1	pound fresh or frozen and thawed scallops
1	pound fresh or frozen and thawed shelled shrimp
1	pound fettuccine or linguine

A loaf of crusty Italian bread and a big bottle of white wine is all you need to complete this meal.

In a dutch oven combine cold water and salt. Add clams. Soak for 15 minutes; drain off water. Rinse clams with cold water. Repeat soaking, draining, and rinsing clams twice or till all of the sand is removed.

In the dutch oven cook garlic in oil till tender but not brown. Add tomatoes; bring to boiling. Add calamari. Return to boiling; reduce heat. Simmer, uncovered, for 20 to 30 minutes. Add parsley, basil, clams, scallops, and shrimp. Cover and simmer for 5 minutes more or till scallops and shrimp are tender and clams open.

Meanwhile cook pasta in boiling water for 8 to 10 minutes or till al dente. Drain. In a large bowl toss together cooked pasta and seafood mixture.

Makes 8 to 10 servings.

Lobster and Clam Fettuccine

This wonderful recipe comes from our friend Paul, who now lives in North Carolina.

4	quarts cold water
1/3	cup salt
24	little neck clams in shells
9	cloves garlic, finely chopped
1/2	cup olive oil
1/2	cup dry white wine
1/3	cup chopped parsley
1	teaspoon salt
1/2	teaspoon pepper
2	1- to 1 1/2-pound live lobsters
1	pound fettuccine
1/2	cup grated Romano cheese

In a dutch oven combine cold water and 1/3 cup salt. Add clams. Soak for 15 minutes; drain off water. Rinse clams with cold water. Repeat soaking, draining, and rinsing clams twice or till all the sand is removed.

In the dutch oven cook garlic in oil till tender but not brown. Stir in wine, parsley, salt, and pepper. Bring to boiling. Add lobsters. Cover and simmer for 15 minutes. Add clams. Cover and cook about 5 minutes more or till lobsters are tender and clams open. Remove lobsters from mixture.

Meanwhile, cook fettuccine in boiling water for 8 to 10 minutes or till al dente. Drain. In a large bowl toss together cooked fettuccine and clam mixture. Sprinkle with grated Romano cheese. Serve with lobsters.

Makes 2 to 4 generous servings.

Pasta Scuita
with Country-Style Salami

1 head cauliflower, cut into bite-size pieces
1 medium onion, chopped
3 cloves garlic, finely chopped
¼ cup olive oil
12 ounces sopressate (country-style salami),
    diced
¼ cup butter or margarine
1 pound ricotta cheese
1 cup milk
1 pound fusilli (twisted spaghetti)
  Salt
  Pepper
¼ cup chopped parsley
1 cup grated Parmesan cheese

In Italy, scuita means "dry sauce." This dish fits that description because it's lightly coated with a ricotta sauce.

In a saucepan cook cauliflower in boiling water about 10 minutes or till crisp-tender. Drain and set aside. In a large skillet cook onion and garlic in oil till onion is tender. Add sopressata. Cook for 2 minutes more. Add cauliflower; heat through.

In a small saucepan melt butter. Stir in ricotta cheese and milk. Cook and stir over medium heat for 2 to 3 minutes or till mixture becomes creamy.

Meanwhile, cook fusilli in boiling water for 15 minutes or till al dente. Drain. In a large bowl toss together pasta, ricotta mixture, and cauliflower mixture. Season with salt and pepper. Sprinkle with parsley and Parmesan cheese.

Makes 4 to 6 servings.

ITALIAN SPECIALTIES

*S*ix simple words can describe this entire chapter: "What are we having for dinner?" When we get together in my mother's kitchen, eventually someone asks this question. That's when the fun begins! Everyone crowds around to lend hands and expertise to the meal. Although we don't always agree, the food is always great.

This chapter reflects the way we cook at home. Most of the recipes have been lovingly prepared over the years by my mother and grandmothers. Some of our long-standing favorites are Marion's Meat Loaf, Grandma's Chicken, and Braciola. Most families have a group of special recipes they turn to again and again. We hope our family favorites will become yours too.

Marion's Spareribs

2	14½-ounce cans chicken broth
1	cup soy sauce
2	teaspoons garlic powder
24	beef spareribs

My mother captivates us every time with her mouthwatering, yet simple, spareribs. These also make great appetizers.

For marinade, in a mixing bowl stir together chicken broth, soy sauce, and garlic powder. Place ribs in a shallow baking pan. Pour marinade over ribs. Marinate ribs in the refrigerator for at least 1 hour, turning occasionally.

Bake in a 350°F oven for 1½ hours or till done. Baste with marinade occasionally during baking. Drain spareribs before serving.

Makes 6 servings.

 ## Sicilian Steak

2	eggs, beaten
2	tablespoons milk
½	cup grated Parmesan cheese
	Dash garlic powder
4	12-ounce beef sirloin steaks
1	cup dry bread crumbs
1	tablespoon olive oil

A very easy recipe that is great for unexpected dinner guests.

In a mixing bowl combine eggs and milk. Stir in Parmesan cheese and garlic powder. Dip steaks into egg mixture. Coat with bread crumbs.

Arrange steaks in a shallow baking pan lightly coated with oil. Bake in a 375°F oven for 10 minutes. Turn steaks and bake for 10 minutes more, or longer if desired.

Makes 4 servings.

Manganaro's Tripe

I dedicate this recipe to tripe lovers, like me. We are few and far between.

3   **pounds beef tripe**
2   **16-ounce cans tomatoes, cut up**
4   **cloves garlic, finely chopped**
2   **tablespoons olive oil**
½   **teaspoon salt**
     Dash ground red pepper

Place tripe in a dutch oven and cover with water. Bring to boiling; reduce heat. Cover and simmer about 50 minutes or till tripe is tender. Drain. When tripe is cool enough to handle, remove excess fat and cut into bite-size pieces.

Meanwhile, in a large saucepan combine tomatoes, garlic, oil, salt, and red pepper. Bring to boiling. Add tripe. Reduce heat. Simmer, uncovered, for 40 minutes or till desired consistency.

Makes about 6 servings.

 ## Crab Quiche

Unlike most quiches, our crab and spinach quiches contain cooked rice and ricotta cheese.

3   **cups water**
½   **cup Arborio or long grain rice**
1   **pound ricotta cheese**
3   **eggs, beaten**
1   **pound mozzarella cheese, chopped**
1   **pound crabmeat**
1   **medium onion, chopped**
     Salt
     Pepper
     Butter or margarine
2   **tablespoons dry Italian-seasoned bread crumbs**
3   **tablespoons milk**

In a large saucepan bring water to boiling. Add rice. Return to boiling; reduce heat. Cover and simmer for 20 to 25 minutes or till rice is tender. Drain. Stir in ricotta cheese, eggs, mozzarella cheese, crabmeat, and onion. Season with salt and pepper.

Butter an 11-inch quiche dish; coat with bread crumbs. Spoon crab mixture into quiche dish. Pour milk over crab mixture (this makes the top brown and crusty after baking). Bake, uncovered, in a 350°F oven for 45 to 50 minutes or till top is golden brown and a knife inserted near the center comes out clean. Let cool for 5 minutes.

Makes 8 servings.

 ## Spinach Quiche

3   cups water
½   cup Arborio or long grain rice
1   pound ricotta cheese
3   eggs, beaten
1   pound mozzarella cheese, chopped
12 cups chopped fresh spinach (about 1 ½ pounds)
    Salt
    Pepper
    Butter or margarine
2   tablespoons dry Italian-seasoned bread crumbs
3   tablespoons milk

We make huge batches of quiche at the store for our lunch customers. We've scaled our recipe down to serve 8 people. You can use any vegetable in place of the spinach.

In a large saucepan bring water to boiling. Add rice. Return to boiling; reduce heat. Cover and simmer for 20 to 25 minutes or till rice is tender. Drain. Stir in ricotta cheese, eggs, mozzarella cheese, and spinach. Season with salt and pepper.

Butter an 11-inch quiche dish; coat with bread crumbs. Spoon spinach mixture into quiche dish. Pour milk over spinach mixture (this makes the top brown and crusty after baking). Bake, uncovered, in a 350°F oven for 45 to 50 minutes or till the top is golden brown and a knife inserted near the center comes out clean. Let cool for 5 minutes.

Makes 8 servings.

❧ Roasted Peppers and Sausages ❧

A good, basic family recipe that my Mother makes.

2   **large onions, sliced**
½   **cup olive oil**
12   **peppers, cut into strips**
1   **pound hot Italian sausage links**
1   **pound sweet Italian sausage links**
     Salt
     Pepper
     Garlic powder

In a medium skillet cook onion in oil till tender. Arrange peppers in a shallow baking pan. Pour onion mixture over peppers. Bake, uncovered, in a 375°F oven for 45 minutes.

Meanwhile, place sausages in a large skillet and fry. Drain off grease from sausages.

Cut sausages into 1-inch pieces and add to pan with peppers. Season with salt, pepper, and garlic powder.

Makes 8 to 10 servings.

❧ Cotechino with Beans ❧

Cotechino is fresh pork sausage that contains pork rind, shoulder meat, cheek meat, and neck meat. It is deliciously seasoned with salt, pepper, nutmeg, and cloves.

1 ½   **pounds cotechino or garlic link sausage**
4   **cloves garlic, finely chopped**
2   **tablespoons olive oil**
2   **16-ounce cans tomatoes, cut up**
1   **16-ounce can red kidney beans, drained**
1   **bunch broccoli, cut into bite-size pieces**
⅓   **cup chopped parsley**
     Salt
     Pepper
1   **pound desired pasta**
½   **cup grated Parmesan cheese**

In a large saucepan cook sausages in boiling water for 35 to 40 minutes or till done. Spoon off fat from water as sausages cook. Drain sausages; cut into ½-inch slices.

Meanwhile, in a large skillet cook garlic in oil till tender but not brown. Add sliced sausage, tomatoes, beans, broccoli, and parsley. Bring to boiling; reduce heat. Simmer, uncovered, for 45 minutes. Season with salt and pepper.

While sausage mixture simmers, cook pasta in boiling water till al dente. Drain. Serve with sausage mixture. Sprinkle with Parmesan cheese.

Makes 4 to 6 servings.

Note: Instead of serving Cotechino with Beans with pasta, we sometimes make polenta as follows: Bring 2¾ cups water to boiling. Stir together 1 cup cornmeal and 1 teaspoon salt. Slowly add to boiling water, stirring constantly. Cook and stir till boiling. Reduce heat. Cook and stir about 20 minutes or till thick. Pour into a 9-inch pie plate. Cover and chill for 30 minutes or till firm. Bake in a 350°F oven for 20 minutes or till hot. Cut into wedges.

Zampone

4 to 6	**pounds zampone (garlic sausage) or Polish sausage**
2	**pounds broccoli, broccoli rabe (a bitter leafy green with tiny yellow buds), or chicory, torn into small pieces**
2	**pounds escarole, torn into small pieces**
9	**cloves garlic, finely chopped**
2	**tablespoons olive oil**
	Dash salt

In a large dutch oven cover zampone with water. Bring to boiling; reduce heat. Simmer for 3 to 4 hours or till done. Drain. Remove skin from meat. Cut meat into ½-inch slices.

Meanwhile, in another dutch oven cover broccoli, broccoli rabe, or chicory with water. Bring to boiling; reduce heat. Simmer for 5 minutes. Add escarole. Return to boiling. Reduce heat and simmer for 5 minutes more. Drain.

While vegetables are cooking, in a saucepan cook garlic in oil till tender but not brown. Add to cooked vegetables. Toss till well coated. Sprinkle with salt.

Arrange sliced meat in the center of a large platter. Surround meat with cooked vegetable mixture.

Makes 12 to 15 servings.

Zampone is a pig's leg stuffed with a zesty mixture of ground pork, garlic, and spices enclosed in a natural casing. The flavors in the pig's leg are wonderful. We purchase our zampone at a local butcher. If you cannot find zampone, you can substitute Polish sausage.

We usually eat this hearty dish during the cold winter months. In some parts of Italy, such as Modena, it is served on New Year's Day. For a real feast with all the trimmings, we serve Zampone with polenta, cooked lentils, and a radicchio and tomato salad.

Sausage and Ricotta Hero Sandwiches

You can use either hot or sweet Italian sausage links for these sandwiches.

10 Italian sausage links (about 2 pounds)
10 club rolls (3- to 4-inches long)
2   pounds ricotta cheese

Place sausages on the unheated rack of a broiler pan. Prick sausages with a fork. Broil about 25 minutes or till done.

Halve rolls lengthwise. Spread ricotta cheese on half of the bread slices. Arrange on baking sheet. Broil for 1 to 2 minutes or till cheese is hot. Top with sausage links. Top with remaining slices of bread. Serve warm.

Makes 10 servings.

Virginia Baked Ham

Virginia ham is a country-style ham that has been dry-salt cured and aged. It is saltier than other hams and has a wonderfully distinctive flavor. If you can't get a Virginia ham, use a 14-pound whole ham with bone instead.

1   14-pound Virginia ham with bone
16 whole cloves
1   cup packed brown sugar
1   15-ounce can pineapple slices, drained
14 maraschino cherries
3   12-ounce cans cola

Place meat, fat side up, on a rack in a shallow baking pan. Cut 16 small criss-crosses over the top of the ham. Stud the center of each criss-cross with 1 clove.

Pat brown sugar evenly over the ham and cover with pineapple slices, securing with toothpicks if necessary. Arrange cherries on top and pour on half of the cola. Insert a meat thermometer in ham.

Bake in a 325°F oven about 4 hours or till thermometer registers 160°F, adding the remaining cola after the first hour. Baste ham occasionally during baking.

Makes about 16 servings.

The Manganaro Italian Family Cookbook

Manganaro's Famous Sandwiches

If I had to name one food that keeps customers coming back to our store, I would say sandwiches. Imported meats, cheeses, sun-dried tomatoes, pesto, artichoke hearts, pickled vegetables, lettuce, and tomatoes are just a few of the fillers you'll find between our bread. I'm listing some of our favorite sandwich combinations so you can make them at home.

- Smoked mozzarella cheese, sun-dried tomatoes, and sopressate

- Turkey, fresh mozzarella cheese, lettuce, tomato, and pesto

- Fresh mozzarella cheese, chunks of Parmesan cheese, olive oil, fresh basil, and sun-dried tomatoes

- Turkey, Sicilian salami, imported provolone cheese, and roasted peppers

- Black Forest ham, Swiss cheese, artichoke hearts, lettuce, and tomatoes

- Special combo—Swiss cheese, ham, lettuce, pickled vegetables (carrots, cauliflower, and peppers), mortadella, cappicola, Genoa salami, cooked salami, prosciutto, and provolone cheese

- Prosciutto and fresh mozzarella cheese

- Veal cutlets and Arugula Salad

- Chicken cutlets, lettuce, and fresh lemon juice

Veal and Peppers

If you're looking for a hearty and aromatic winter meal, this is it.

1 large onion, chopped
¼ cup olive oil
½ cup dry white wine
2 pounds boneless veal, cut into chunks
6 bay leaves
½ teaspoon garlic powder
Salt
Pepper
8 green or sweet red peppers, sliced
2 cloves garlic, finely chopped
½ cup olive oil

In a large saucepan cook onion in ¼ cup oil till tender. Stir in wine. Add veal, bay leaves, and garlic powder. Bring to boiling; reduce heat. Simmer, uncovered, for 1 hour or till desired consistency. Remove bay leaves. Season with salt and pepper.

Meanwhile, in a large skillet cook sliced peppers and garlic in ½ cup oil till tender. Serve with veal mixture.

Makes 8 servings.

 ## Veal Parmigiano

What can I say? This is a true classic, one which my whole family loves.

2 pounds veal cutlets, cut into 6 portions
6 eggs, beaten
½ cup milk
¼ teaspoon salt
¼ teaspoon pepper
4 cups dry bread crumbs
½ cup grated Parmesan cheese
2 cups olive oil
2 pounds mozzarella cheese, sliced
8 cups Marinara Sauce

Pound veal cutlets with the flat side of a meat mallet to ¼-inch thickness. In a mixing bowl combine eggs, milk, salt, and pepper. In another bowl combine dry bread crumbs and

Parmesan cheese. Dip each piece of veal into egg mixture. Coat with bread crumb mixture.

In a large skillet cook veal in hot oil for 2 minutes per side or till done. Arrange veal in a shallow baking pan. Top with sliced mozzarella cheese. Pour about 1 cup of the Marinara Sauce over cheese and veal.

Bake, uncovered, in a 350°F oven for 10 minutes or till cheese melts. Meanwhile, heat remaining sauce in a saucepan. Serve sauce with the veal. Spaghetti is the perfect pasta to accompany Veal Parmigiano.

Makes 6 servings.

 ## Stuffed Roast Veal

2	ounces bread sticks
1	8-pound boneless veal roast, butterflied
4	ounces prosciutto, sliced
4	cloves garlic, finely chopped
½	cup pine nuts
5	hard-cooked eggs, sliced
	Coarse cracked pepper
	Garlic powder

A butterflied veal roast is split all the way through the center, then spread flat for easier stuffing. Ask your butcher to butterfly the veal roast when you buy it.

Crumble bread sticks into a bowl. Cover with warm water. Soak for 2 minutes; drain well. Lay meat as flat as possible. Layer with prosciutto, garlic, pine nuts, sliced eggs, and bread sticks. Season with coarse cracked pepper.

To roll the roast, start at the short side of the roast and roll up jelly-roll style. Secure the meat with a sturdy string. Tie the roast crosswise at several places to prevent it from coming unrolled during cooking.

Rub outside of roast with garlic powder. Insert a meat thermometer. Place meat in a large shallow roasting pan. Roast in a 350°F oven for 2½ to 3 hours or till meat thermometer registers 170°F. Let meat stand for 15 minutes. Remove the string before carving.

Makes 20 servings.

Veal Marsala

This special-occasion recipe is rich tasting and extremely easy to make.

2 **pounds veal cutlets, cut into 6 portions**
1 **cup olive oil**
½ **cup butter or margarine**
2 **cups flour**
2 **cups sliced fresh mushrooms**
1 **cup marsala or dry sherry**

Pound veal with the flat side of a meat mallet to ¼-inch thickness. In a large skillet heat oil and butter till butter melts.

Coat veal with flour. Add to skillet. Cook over medium-high heat about 2 minutes per side or till veal is done. Remove veal, reserving skillet drippings. Cover veal and keep warm in oven set at a low temperature.

In the same skillet cook mushrooms in reserved drippings till tender. Add marsala or sherry. Bring to boiling; reduce heat. Simmer, uncovered, till liquid is reduced to half. Pour over veal.

Makes 6 servings.

 # Roast Veal

During the winter, my mother serves us a huge dinner each Sunday. This dish is usually the main attraction.

1 **8-pound boneless veal roast**
¼ **teaspoon garlic powder**
¼ **teaspoon pepper**
5 **bay leaves**
1 **medium onion, sliced**
8 **strips of bacon**
2 **16-ounce cans whole white potatoes, drained**
12 **pearl onions or 6 medium onions, quartered**
¼ **cup flour**

Place roast in a shallow roasting pan. Sprinkle with garlic powder and pepper. Arrange bay leaves on top of roast. Cover with onion slices and top with bacon.

Insert a meat thermometer in roast. Bake, uncovered, in a 350°F oven for 30 minutes. Remove bacon slices. Arrange potatoes and onions around roast. Continue cooking for 2 ½ to 3 hours or till thermometer registers 170°F.

Remove meat and vegetables from pan, reserving drippings. Keep warm. Stir flour into pan drippings till smooth. Return to oven till mixture is thickened and bubbly. Serve with meat and vegetables.

Makes 16 to 20 servings.

Braciola

2 ounces bread sticks
4 ounces prosciutto or Canadian bacon, finely chopped
4 ounces provolone cheese, shredded
½ cup pine nuts or chopped walnuts
¼ cup olive oil
½ teaspoon dried parsley
¼ teaspoon salt
¼ teaspoon pepper
1 pound beef tenderloin, cut into 4 pieces
4 garlic cloves, finely chopped
¼ cup olive oil
2 16-ounce cans tomatoes, cut up
1 6-ounce can tomato paste
6 large basil leaves

We serve this fabulous dish on special occasions. When you remove the meat from the sauce, it should fall apart and literally melt in your mouth.

Crumble bread sticks into a mixing bowl. Cover with warm water. Let soak for 2 to 3 minutes or till soft. Drain. Stir in prosciutto, provolone, nuts, ¼ cup oil, parsley, salt, and pepper. Set aside.

Pound beef with a meat mallet to ¼-inch thickness. Spoon prosciutto mixture onto beef. Starting at the short side, roll up meat jelly-roll style. Tie beef rolls with a sturdy string.

In a large saucepan cook garlic in ¼ cup oil till tender but not brown. Add beef rolls to hot oil. Cook over high heat till meat is brown, turning to brown evenly. Stir in tomatoes, tomato paste, and basil. Bring to boiling; reduce heat. Simmer, uncovered, for 1 hour or till sauce is desired consistency and meat is tender. Remove meat from tomato mixture, and remove the string. Serve meat with tomato mixture.

Makes 4 servings.

Marion's Meat Loaf

My mother's meat loaf is so outrageously good that it can even be chilled and served as a pâté.

12 slices bread, torn into pieces
7 eggs, beaten
¼ cup chopped parsley
1 tablespoon salt
1½ teaspoons pepper
¼ teaspoon celery seed
¼ teaspoon onion powder
2 pounds ground beef
1 cup grated Parmesan cheese
3 tablespoons olive oil
1 15-ounce can or jar of brown gravy

Place torn bread in a large mixing bowl; cover with warm water. Let bread soak for 2 minutes; drain. Add eggs, parsley, salt, pepper, celery seed, and onion powder to bread mixture. Add ground beef and Parmesan cheese. Mix well.

Press meat mixture into a 12 × 7½ × 2-inch baking dish lightly coated with oil. Bake in a 350°F oven for 1½ hours or till done. Drain off fat, if desired. Pour brown gravy over meat loaf. Continue baking for 5 minutes more or till gravy is heated through.

Makes 8 to 12 servings.

 Italian Meatballs

You can serve these meatballs alone or spoon sauce over them. Either way, they are delicious.

7 eggs, beaten
2 cups dry Italian-seasoned bread crumbs
¼ cup dried parsley
4 cloves garlic, finely chopped
½ teaspoon salt
½ teaspoon pepper
½ teaspoon onion powder
2 pounds ground beef
2 cups grated Romano cheese
½ cup olive oil

In a large mixing bowl combine eggs, bread crumbs, parsley, garlic, salt, pepper, and onion powder. Add beef and grated

Romano cheese. Mix well. Shape meat mixture into 1½- to 2-inch meatballs (you should have about 16 meatballs).

In a large skillet slowly cook half of the meatballs in oil, turning to brown evenly. Drain meatballs on paper towels, reserving oil. Add more oil, if necessary, before cooking and draining remaining meatballs as directed.

Makes 8 servings.

Marion's Meatballs: Prepare Italian Meatballs as directed, omitting bread crumbs, garlic, and onion powder. Soak 9 slices of bread in warm water for 2 to 3 minutes or till soft. Drain well. Add bread, 1 large chopped onion, and 1 teaspoon garlic salt to meat mixture. Continue as directed.

Savory Stuffed Peppers

6	medium green or red sweet peppers
	Salt
2	eggs, beaten
8	ounces ground beef
1	cup cooked rice
1	small onion, chopped
¼	cup pine nuts or chopped walnuts
2	tablespoons grated Parmesan cheese
1	teaspoon dried parsley
½	teaspoon salt
½	teaspoon pepper
½	teaspoon dried basil, crushed

We serve these every Monday at our store. Most customers eat them with a small salad.

Cut tops off of peppers; reserve tops. Remove seeds and membranes. If desired, cook the whole peppers, uncovered, in boiling water for 5 minutes. Invert on paper towels to drain well. Sprinkle insides lightly with salt.

In a mixing bowl stir together eggs, beef, rice, onion, nuts, Parmesan, parsley, salt, pepper, and basil.

Spoon meat mixture into peppers. Place tops on peppers and arrange in a shallow baking dish. Bake in a 375°F oven for 1 hour or till meat is done and peppers are tender.

Makes 6 servings.

Italian Main Dish Specialties

Lemon Chicken

Prepare to pucker up. Our lemon-basted chicken is deliciously tangy.

1	2 ½- to 3-pound chicken, cut up
1	cup olive oil
¾	cup lemon juice
4	cloves garlic, chopped
2	teaspoons dried oregano, crushed
½	teaspoon salt
½	teaspoon pepper

Rinse chicken; pat dry with paper towels. For marinade, in a mixing bowl combine oil, lemon juice, garlic, oregano, salt, and pepper. Place chicken in a shallow baking pan. Pour marinade over chicken and allow to marinate in the refrigerator at least 2 hours or overnight, turning chicken pieces occasionally.

Bake in a 350°F oven about 50 minutes or till chicken is done, basting occasionally with marinade. Drain before serving.

Makes 4 servings.

 ## Spinach Stuffed Chickens

One day my sister Linda was trying to duplicate my grandmother's stuffing. In a flash of brilliance she added creamed spinach to the basic recipe. We love the results.

2	10-ounce packages frozen chopped spinach
2	3-ounce packages cream cheese
1 ½	pounds mozzarella cheese, finely chopped
1 ½	cups grated Parmesan cheese
8	eggs, beaten
1	pound fully cooked ham, chopped
4	ounces prosciutto, chopped
⅓	cup chopped parsley
2	ounces bread sticks, crumbled
1	teaspoon garlic powder
½	teaspoon salt
½	teaspoon pepper
2	7-pound capons or one 10-pound turkey Olive oil

In a medium saucepan cook spinach according to package directions; drain. In a large mixing bowl stir together hot spinach and cream cheese till well combined. Add mozzarella and Parmesan cheeses, eggs, ham, prosciutto, parsley, bread sticks, garlic powder, salt, and pepper.

Rinse capons or turkey; pat dry with paper towels, and fill with spinach mixture. (Or omit birds and transfer stuffing to a covered casserole dish. Bake about 45 minutes or till heated through.) Skewer neck skin to back. Tuck drumsticks under tail skin. Twist wing tips under.

Place birds, breast side up, on a rack in a shallow roasting pan. Brush skin with oil. Insert a meat thermometer. Roast, uncovered, in a 350°F oven about 3 hours for the capons, 4 hours for the turkey, or till thermometer registers 180°F to 185°F. Remove from oven; cover loosely with foil. Let stand 15 to 20 minutes before carving.

Makes 12 to 14 servings.

 # Grandma's Chicken

2	pounds boneless, skinless chicken breasts
6	medium potatoes, peeled and sliced ¼-inch thick
1	large onion, sliced
¼	cup olive oil
2	cups dry bread crumbs
¼	cup butter or margarine, melted
¼	teaspoon dried oregano, crushed
	Salt
	Pepper

Sometimes we make this with 12 or 18 chicken drumsticks instead of chicken breasts.

Rinse chicken; pat dry with paper towels. In a mixing bowl toss together the potatoes, onion, and oil. Line a shallow baking dish with potato mixture, sprinkle with bread crumbs, and top with chicken. Brush chicken with melted butter. Sprinkle with oregano.

Bake in a 375°F oven for 1¼ hours or till chicken is done and potatoes are tender. Season with salt and pepper.

Makes 6 servings.

Stuffed Turkey

At Thanksgiving, we cook for friends and family, so we use a 24-pound turkey. If your family is smaller, you can halve the stuffing ingredients and use a 12-pound turkey.

12	slices bread, torn
16	eggs
1	cup chopped parsley
2	teaspoons salt
2	teaspoons pepper
3	pounds Italian link sausage
2	medium onions, chopped
1½	pounds mushrooms, chopped
½	cup olive oil
1	cup chopped parsley
1	24-pound turkey
1	cup melted butter or margarine

For stuffing, place torn bread in a large mixing bowl; cover with warm water. Let bread soak for 2 minutes; drain. Add eggs, chopped parsley, salt, and pepper.

Remove casing from sausage; break sausage into pieces. In a large skillet cook sausage, onions, and mushrooms in oil till sausage is done. Stir in parsley. Pour sausage mixture over bread mixture in large bowl. Stir till well combined.

Rinse turkey; pat dry with paper towels. Season the body cavity with salt. Spoon stuffing into neck cavity. Skewer neck skin to back. Spoon stuffing into body cavity. Place any remaining stuffing in a casserole; cover and chill. Tuck drumsticks under tail skin. Twist wing tips under.

Place turkey, breast side up, on a rack in a shallow roasting pan. Drizzle with butter. Insert a meat thermometer in the center of the inside thigh muscle, making sure the bulb of the thermometer does not touch the bone. Roast turkey in a 375°F oven for 10 hours or till thermometer registers 180°F to 185°F, basting occasionally. Place the covered casserole with stuffing in oven during the last hour or roasting.

Remove turkey from oven. Cover with foil and let stand 20 minutes before carving.

Makes about 30 servings.

Chicken Cacciatore

2 ounces dried mushrooms
1 2½- to 3-pound chicken, cut up
2 16-ounce cans tomatoes, cut up
1 medium onion, chopped
½ cup dry white wine
4 bay leaves
¼ teaspoon salt
¼ teaspoon pepper
¼ teaspoon garlic powder
1 pound rigatoni (ridged pasta tubes)

This is another store specialty that is extremely popular with our customers. Serve it with a light green salad and a loaf of crusty bread.

Place mushrooms in a bowl, cover with warm water, and soak about 5 minutes or till tender. Drain and slice mushrooms.

Rinse chicken; pat dry with paper towels. Arrange chicken pieces in a shallow baking pan. Add mushrooms, tomatoes, onion, wine, bay leaves, salt, pepper, and garlic powder.

Bake, uncovered, in a 350°F oven for 40 to 45 minutes or till chicken is done, basting occasionally with the tomato mixture. Remove bay leaves.

Meanwhile, cook rigatoni in boiling water for 15 minutes or till al dente. Drain and serve with the chicken.

Makes 4 servings.

Pan-Fried Shrimp

2 pounds large shrimp in shells
¼ cup butter or margarine
Salt
Pepper
Garlic powder

These succulent peel-and-eat shellfish are messy, so serve them on a table covered with newspaper. Complete the feast with cooked macaroni, corn on the cob, and french fries.

In a large skillet (preferably a cast iron skillet) cook shrimp in butter for 5 to 6 minutes or till shrimp turn pink. Season with salt, pepper, and garlic powder. Let each person shell his shrimp at the table.

Makes 4 to 6 servings.

Bacon-Wrapped Shrimp

Large sea scallops are a delicious alternative to the shrimp.

12 jumbo shrimp, peeled and deveined
12 slices of bacon
2 pounds fresh spinach
Olive oil

Wrap each shrimp in 1 slice of bacon. Secure with a toothpick. Arrange in a single layer on a baking sheet. Bake in a 400°F oven for 7 to 8 minutes or till shrimp are pink and bacon is crisp.

Meanwhile, cook spinach in a large saucepan or dutch oven. Drain and transfer spinach to a serving platter. Drizzle lightly with oil. Arrange bacon-wrapped shrimp on bed of spinach.

Makes 2 or 3 servings.

Garlic Scallops with Sun-Dried Tomatoes

5 large cloves garlic, finely chopped
1/4 cup olive oil
1/4 pound marinated sun-dried tomatoes, drained
2 tablespoons capers, drained
1 pound sea scallops
8 fresh whole basil leaves or 1 teaspoon dried basil, crushed
Salt
Pepper

In a large skillet cook garlic in oil till tender but not brown. Add sun-dried tomatoes and capers; cook for 1 to 2 minutes. Add scallops; cook and stir about 5 minutes or till tender. Add basil. Season with salt and pepper.

Makes 3 servings.

Fried Soft Shell Crabs

- 12 soft shell crabs
- 4   eggs, beaten
- ¼   cup milk
- ½   teaspoon salt
- ½   teaspoon pepper
- 3   cups flour
- 2   cups olive oil

To clean crabs, grasp each crab between the back legs. Cut across the body about ½ inch behind the eyes, removing the face. Life the pointed soft top shell on one side. Using your fingers, push up the spongy portions on the exposed side and pull them off. Replace the soft top shell over the body. Repeat on the other side of the crab. Turn crab over. Pull up the apron-shape piece and discard. Thoroughly rinse crabs under cold running water to remove the yellow substance. Handle crabs gently while cleaning them. Pat dry with paper towels.

In a mixing bowl combine eggs, milk, salt, and pepper. Dip each crab in egg mixture. Coat with flour.

In a large skillet fry crabs in a single layer in hot oil for 2 to 3 minutes or till golden brown. Turn carefully. Fry for 2 to 3 minutes more or till golden brown. Drain on paper towels. Repeat, frying remaining crabs in a single layer in skillet. Keep fried crabs warm in a 300°F oven, if desired.

Makes 6 servings.

Crabs

The most common types of crab marketed today are blue, Dungeness, king, snow, and stone crabs. Soft-shell crabs are blue crabs that have shed their hard shells. When buying live crabs, choose active ones that smell fresh. Cook live crabs as soon as possible after you purchase them. To store them for a short time, place them in a sink or bathtub filled with cold water, or on wet newspapers in an insulated cooler that is half-filled with ice. Before cooking, make sure crabs are still alive.

Capellini Fritti

This recipe for fried angel hair pasta can take center stage for breakfast, brunch, or a summer dinner. Serve it with an arugula salad and garlic bread.

1   pound angel hair pasta
1   6-ounce can crabmeat
6   eggs
3   tablespoons milk
    Salt
    Pepper
4   tablespoons olive oil

Cook pasta in boiling water for 5 to 6 minutes or till al dente; drain. Meanwhile, drain, flake, and remove the cartilage from crab. In a large bowl combine cooked pasta, crabmeat, eggs, milk, salt, and pepper. Toss together.

Heat oil in a 12-inch skillet over medium heat. Add egg and pasta mixture, spreading evenly in skillet. As eggs set, run a spatula around edge of the skillet. Lift the eggs to allow the uncooked portion to flow underneath. When eggs are set but still shiny, invert onto a serving platter.

Makes 6 servings.

Crab Cakes

My family thinks of these as a great summer entree. Serve them with buttered corn on the cob and a crisp salad.

4   eggs, beaten
1   pound frozen crabmeat, thawed
1   pound ricotta cheese
1   pound mozzarella cheese, chopped
½   teaspoon salt
½   teaspoon pepper
¼   teaspoon garlic powder
¼   teaspoon dried thyme, crushed
1   medium onion, finely chopped
2   tablespoons olive oil
2   cups dry bread crumbs
1   cup olive oil

In a large mixing bowl stir together eggs, crabmeat, ricotta and mozzarella cheeses, salt, pepper, garlic powder, and thyme.

In a small skillet cook onion in 2 tablespoons oil till tender. Add to crab mixture. Stir till well combined. Shape mixture into 12 small or 6 large patties. Coat patties evenly with bread crumbs.

In a large skillet fry half of the patties in 1 cup hot oil for 2 to 3 minutes per side or till golden brown. Drain on paper towels. Fry and drain remaining patties as directed.

Makes 6 servings.

 # Fried Calamari

3 **pounds calamari, cleaned and cut up**
2 **cups flour**
4 **cups olive oil**
   Salt
   Pepper
1 **lemon, quartered**

We eat these crispy critters the way other people eat potato chips.

Coat calamari with flour. Fry pieces of calamari, a few at a time, in hot oil (375°F) about 1½ minutes or till golden brown, turning once. Drain on paper towels. Keep fried calamari warm in a 300°F oven while frying remaining calamari. Season with salt and pepper. Serve with lemon.

Makes 12 servings.

 ## Cleaning Squid

Soak squid in a pot of cold water for 20 minutes. Drain. Pull off the tentacles from each squid. The tentacles come away attached to the inside pulp of the squid. Cut the tentacles just above the eyes. Discard the pulpy matter. Squeeze off the tiny beak at the base of the tentacles. Wash the tentacles in several changes of cold water. Pat dry with paper towels. Remove the floppy, cellophane-like bone from the sac. Peel off the sac's outer skin. Rinse the sac under cold running water. Pat dry with paper towels. Continue as directed in the recipes.

❧ Calamari in Tomato Sauce ❧

Calamari, also known as squid, is very tender. To keep it from becoming rubbery, cook it either very quickly over high heat or slowly over low heat. In this recipe the squid is cooked slowly.

8   cloves garlic, finely chopped
¼   cup olive oil
4   16-ounce cans tomatoes, cut up
3   pounds fresh calamari, cleaned and cut up
⅓   cup chopped fresh basil
⅓   cup chopped parsley
1   teaspoon salt
½   teaspoon pepper
    Dash ground red pepper
2   pounds desired pasta

In a large saucepan cook garlic in oil till tender but not brown. Add tomatoes. Bring to boiling; reduce heat. Simmer, uncovered, for 10 minutes. Add calamari, basil, parsley, salt, pepper, and red pepper. Simmer, uncovered, for 25 minutes, or till calamari is tender, stirring occasionally.

Meanwhile, cook pasta in boiling water till al dente. Drain. Serve with squid mixture.

Makes 12 servings.

❧ Grandma's Stuffed Calamari ❧

Instead of serving flounder or cod for dinner tonight, surprise your family with this delicacy.

2   eggs, beaten
2   cups dry bread crumbs
¼   cup chopped parsley
½   cup pine nuts
¼   cup grated Romano cheese
½   teaspoon garlic powder
½   teaspoon pepper
3 to 4 pounds whole calamari, cleaned
¼   cup olive oil
2   16-ounce cans tomatoes, cut up
        Salt
        Pepper

For stuffing, in a mixing bowl stir together eggs, bread crumbs, parsley, pine nuts, Romano cheese, garlic powder, and pepper.

Rinse the sac of each calamari under cold running water. Gently pat dry with paper towels. Fill the sacs loosely with the stuffing. Secure with toothpicks, if necessary.

In a large skillet quickly fry the stuffed calamari in a single layer in hot oil till brown. Turn calamari carefully to brown on the other side. Add tomatoes. Season with salt and pepper. Bring to boiling; reduce heat. Simmer, uncovered, for 15 to 30 minutes or till calamari is tender.

Makes 12 servings.

Grandma's Stuffed Calamari #2: Prepare Grandma's Stuffed Calamari as directed, substituting grated Parmesan cheese for the Romano cheese and 3 stalks of finely chopped celery for the pine nuts. Continue as directed.

 # Fried Flounder

2   **pounds fresh or frozen flounder fillets**
6   **eggs, beaten**
½   **cup milk**
½   **teaspoon salt**
½   **teaspoon pepper**
½   **teaspoon dried parsley**
3   **cups dry Italian-seasoned bread crumbs**
2   **cups olive oil**

Thaw flounder, if frozen. Cut flounder into 6 portions. Rinse and pat dry with paper towels.

In a mixing bowl combine eggs, milk, salt, pepper, and parsley. Dip fish in egg mixture. Coat with bread crumbs. Fry flounder in hot oil till golden brown. Allow 3 to 4 minutes for ½ inch thickness or 5 to 6 minutes for 1 inch thickness. Turn and fry till fish is golden brown and flakes easily with a fork.

Makes 6 servings.

Codfish Genovese

1 pound salted, dried codfish
4 cloves garlic, finely chopped
1 cup olive oil
1/3 cup chopped parsley
2 tablespoons tomato paste
1 teaspoon pepper
1/4 teaspoon salt
1 pound desired pasta (optional)

Place codfish in a large bowl. Cover with water. Cover and soak in the refrigerator for 3 days, changing water each day. Drain.

In a large skillet cook garlic in oil till tender but not brown. Add codfish, parsley, tomato paste, pepper, and salt. Bring to boiling; reduce heat. Simmer, uncovered, for 1 hour.

Meanwhile, if desired, cook pasta in boiling water till al dente. Drain and serve with codfish mixture.

Makes 4 servings.

 Fried Codfish (Baccala)

1 pound salted, dried codfish
1 cup flour
2 tablespoons grated Parmesan cheese
1 teaspoon pepper
1/4 teaspoon salt
1/4 teaspoon garlic powder
1/2 cup water
2 cups olive oil

Place codfish in a large bowl. Cover with water. Cover and soak in the refrigerator for 3 days, changing water each day. Drain.

For batter, in a mixing bowl stir together flour, Parmesan cheese, pepper, salt, and garlic powder. Add water. Stir till well combined. Dip each piece of codfish into batter. Fry codfish in hot oil for 2 minutes per side or till golden brown. Drain on paper towels. Serve with lemon or Marinara Sauce.

Makes 8 to 10 servings.

❦ Bianca's Codfish (Baccala) Stew ❦

2	pounds salted, dried codfish
4	medium potatoes, sliced
4	stalks celery, sliced
1	large onion, sliced
¼	cup olive oil
1	16-ounce can tomatoes, cut up
½	cup pitted ripe olives, quartered
½	cup dry white wine
2	tablespoons pine nuts or chopped walnuts
1	tablespoon dried parsley
1	teaspoon crushed red pepper
½	teaspoon salt
½	teaspoon pepper

Place codfish in a large bowl. Cover with water. Cover and soak in the refrigerator for 3 days, changing water each day. Drain.

In a large saucepan cook potatoes, celery, and onion in oil till onion is tender. Add tomatoes, olives, wine, nuts, parsley, red pepper, salt, and pepper. Bring to boiling; reduce heat.

Simmer, uncovered, for 15 to 20 minutes or till potatoes are just tender. Add codfish. Simmer for 10 minutes more or till codfish and vegetables are tender.

Makes 6 servings.

❧ Filet of Sole di Pomodori ❧

*Those of you watching
your weight can prepare
this recipe without olive
oil for a great tasting,
low-calorie main dish.*

½ cup olive oil
1 small onion, thinly sliced
2 16-ounce cans tomatoes, cut up
2 pounds sole filets
  Salt
  Pepper
  Dried oregano, crushed

Coat a shallow baking pan with oil. Arrange onions in greased baking pan. Add tomatoes and top with sole fillets. Season with salt, pepper, and oregano.

Bake, uncovered, in a 375°F oven for 35 to 40 minutes or till fish flakes easily when tested with a fork.

Makes 6 servings.

❧ Ham and Cheese Calzones ❧

*We make these special
pocket sandwiches every
Friday at the store.
Bianca, one of our cooks,
was responsible for
perfecting the recipe.*

2 to 2 ½ cups flour
1 package active dry yeast
1 teaspoon salt
1 cup water
½ cup butter or margarine
1 egg, beaten
4 ounces fully cooked ham, chopped
8 ounces ricotta cheese
6 ounces mozzarella cheese, shredded
¼ cup grated Parmesan cheese
4 cups olive oil

For dough, in a mixing bowl stir together 1 cup flour, yeast, and salt. In a saucepan heat water and butter just till warm (115°F to 120°F) and butter is almost melted; stir constantly. Add to flour mixture. Stir vigorously till well combined. Stir in as much of the remaining flour as you can.

Turn dough out onto a lightly floured surface. Knead in enough remaining flour to make a moderately stiff dough that is smooth and elastic (6 to 8 minutes total). Shape into a ball. Place in a greased bowl; turn once to grease surface. Cover and let rise in a warm place till double (30 to 45 minutes).

For filling, in a mixing bowl stir together egg, ham, ricotta, mozzarella, and Parmesan cheeses. Set aside.

Punch dough down. Cover and let rest for 10 minutes. Divide dough into 8 portions and roll out each into a 7-inch circle. Spoon about 2 rounded tablespoons filling onto half of each circle of dough. Fold dough over filling, fold under edges, and pinch to seal.

Fry calzones, a few at a time, in hot oil for 3 to 4 minutes or till golden brown. Drain on paper towels.

Makes 8 calzones.

 Eggplant Rollatini

12	slices fried eggplant
12	slices mozzarella cheese
12	slices prosciutto or Canadian bacon
8	ounces ricotta cheese
	Fresh ground pepper
4	cups Meat Sauce or Marinara Sauce

This is an economical but elegant main dish. Try it the next time you're in a "what can I fix for dinner?" quandary.

Fry eggplant as directed in recipe for Eggplant Parmesan. When eggplant is cool enough to handle, layer 1 slice of eggplant with 1 slice of mozzarella and 1 slice of prosciutto. Spoon some ricotta cheese over prosciutto. Sprinkle with pepper.

Roll up eggplant, jelly-roll style, around cheese and meat. Secure with a toothpick. Repeat with remaining eggplant, cheese, and meat.

Arrange eggplant rolls in shallow baking pan. Bake in a 400°F oven about 15 minutes or till heated through. Meanwhile, heat sauce in a saucepan. Serve with eggplant rolls.

Makes 4 servings.

Eggplant Parmesan

This famous Manganaro classic is a hit with the lunch crowd at our store. Serve it at home with crusty Italian bread.

3	large eggplants
2	cups flour
5	eggs
½	cup milk
1	tablespoon grated Parmesan cheese
¼	teaspoon salt
¼	teaspoon pepper
1	cup olive oil
1	pound mozzarella cheese, sliced
6	cups Marinara Sauce

Peel eggplants; slice lengthwise into ½-inch slices. Coat slices with flour. In a mixing bowl combine eggs, milk, Parmesan cheese, salt, and pepper.

Dip eggplant into egg mixture. Fry in hot oil about 2 minutes per side or till golden brown. Drain on paper towels.

To assemble, arrange fried eggplant in a single layer in a large shallow baking pan. Top with mozzarella cheese.

Bake in a 350°F oven for 5 minutes or till cheese melts. Meanwhile, heat Marinara Sauce in a saucepan. Serve with baked eggplant mixture.

Makes 12 servings.

RISOTTO

When we get in the mood for rice . . . watch out! We eat it with the same abandon as its lip-smacking cousin, pasta. At our house, rice always means risotto.

Risotto is an Italian technique, unlike any other method of preparing rice. The objective is to have the rice slowly absorb the cooking liquid until it swells and becomes creamy. Risottos can take on a variety of flavors, depending on the ingredients you add.

We always use Arborio rice when making risotto. Arborio is an Italian premium rice classified as "superfino," which means that it produces the plumpest, largest grains when cooked. Arborio is readily available at Italian or specialty food shops. And Arborio is so easy to use that I have never undercooked or overcooked it; it has always turned out perfectly.

Neapolitan Rice Balls

8	cups water
1	pound Arborio or long grain rice
8	ounces mozzarella cheese, shredded or finely chopped
¼	cup butter or margarine
¼	cup grated Parmesan cheese
½	teaspoon pepper
2	eggs, beaten
4	ounces mozzarella cheese, cubed
1 to 2	cups dry bread crumbs
3	cups olive oil
	Marinara Sauce (optional)

These are made all over Italy but especially in such places as Naples, Amalfi, and Sicily. They are wonderful by themselves or smothered in Marinara Sauce.

In a large saucepan bring water to boiling. Add rice. Return to boiling; reduce heat. Simmer, uncovered, for 20 to 30 minutes or till rice is tender. Drain thoroughly.

Meanwhile, in a large mixing bowl combine shredded mozzarella cheese, butter, Parmesan cheese, and pepper. Stir hot rice into cheese mixture. Add eggs, one at a time, stirring till well combined. Cover and chill for 24 hours (this makes rice easier to handle).

To make rice balls, with moist hands form the chilled rice mixture into balls about 3 to 4 inches in diameter, inserting 1 or 2 pieces of mozzarella cheese into the center of each ball. Make sure cheese is completely encased in rice mixture.

Coat rice balls evenly with bread crumbs. Fry rice balls in hot oil about 3 minutes or till golden brown and drain on paper towels. Serve with Marinara Sauce, if desired.

Makes 7 to 10 rice balls.

Sicilian Rice Balls: Prepare Neapolitan Rice Balls as directed, omitting the mozzarella. For the filling, in a saucepan cook 8 ounces of ground beef; drain. Stir in one 8-ounce can tomato puree, one 8-ounce can drained peas, and dash salt and pepper. Bring to boiling; reduce heat. Simmer, uncovered, for 5 minutes. Spoon 1 to 2 tablespoons meat mixture into the middle of each rice ball. Continue as directed.

Marion's Risotto

This version of my mother's risotto is flavored with dried mushrooms, sausage, and saffron.

2 ½ ounces dried mushrooms
1   pound Italian sausage
1   medium onion, chopped
2   cups Arborio or long grain rice
6   cups water
½   teaspoon salt
¼   teaspoon pepper
½   teaspoon thread saffron, crushed
1   cup grated Parmesan cheese

Place mushrooms in a small bowl; cover with warm water and let stand about 5 minutes or till soft. Drain mushrooms. Meanwhile, in a large saucepan cook sausage and onion till sausage is brown and onion is tender. Stir in rice. Add water, salt, and pepper. Add mushrooms. Bring to boiling.

Cook and stir over low heat till all the liquid is evaporated. Stir in saffron. The rice is done when it is tender. (If necessary, add more water during cooking.) Stir in grated Parmesan cheese.

Makes 6 servings.

 # Vongole Risotto

Clams are a wonderful addition to basic risotto. We use canned minced clams because they blend nicely into the cooked rice mixture.

3   7 ½-ounce cans minced clams
5   cloves garlic, finely chopped
2   tablespoons olive oil
2   cups Arborio or long grain rice
6   cups water
⅓   cup chopped parsley
½   teaspoon salt
¼   teaspoon pepper
1   cup grated Romano cheese

Drain clams, reserving juice. In a large saucepan cook garlic in oil till tender but not brown. Stir in rice. Add water, reserved clam juice, chopped parsley, salt, and pepper. Bring to boiling.

Cook and stir over low heat till all the liquid is evaporated. The rice is done when it is tender. (If necessary, add more water during cooking.) Stir in minced clams and grated Romano cheese; heat through.

Makes 6 servings.

Risotto with Marinara Sauce

7   cloves garlic, finely chopped
¼   cup olive oil
2   2-pound cans tomatoes, cut up
1   teaspoon salt
1   teaspoon dried oregano
½   teaspoon garlic powder
½   teaspoon pepper
6   cups water
2   cups Arborio or long grain rice
1   cup grated Parmesan cheese

My sister Nina loves this risotto. It is one of her favorite childhood recipes.

For marinara sauce, in a large skillet cook garlic in oil till tender but not brown. Add tomatoes, salt, oregano, garlic powder, and pepper. Bring to boiling; reduce heat. Simmer, uncovered, for 20 to 30 minutes or till desired consistency.

Meanwhile, in a large saucepan bring water to boiling. Add rice. Cook and stir over low heat till all the liquid is evaporated. The rice is done when it is tender. (If necessary, add more water during cooking.) Stir in marinara sauce. Sprinkle with Parmesan cheese.

Makes 6 servings.

Baked Risotto with Marinara Sauce and Three Cheeses: Prepare Risotto with Marinara Sauce as directed, but stir 1½ pounds diced mozzarella cheese and 8 ounces ricotta cheese into rice and marinara sauce mixture. Transfer to a casserole dish. Top with fresh basil leaves. Bake, uncovered, in a 350°F oven for 20 minutes or till heated through. Sprinkle with Parmesan cheese.

Makes 6 to 8 servings.

Risotto

114

✑ Risotto with Chicken Giblets ✑

We sometimes stir 1 ½ cups leftover cooked chicken into the rice mixture before serving.

8	ounces chicken giblets, chopped
1	medium onion, chopped
1	cup chopped fresh mushrooms
½	cup butter or margarine
2	cups Arborio or long grain rice
6	cups chicken broth
½	teaspoon salt
¼	teaspoon pepper
1	beaten egg
½	cup grated Parmesan cheese

In a large saucepan cook giblets, onion, and mushrooms in butter till tender. Stir in rice. Add chicken broth, salt, and pepper. Bring to boiling.

Cook and stir over low heat till all of the liquid is evaporated. The rice is done when it is tender. (If necessary, add more broth during cooking.) Remove from heat. Stir in egg and grated Parmesan cheese.

Makes 6 servings.

✑ Risotto with Asparagus and Fontina ✑

This is a special-occasion risotto that I once prepared for a friend's wedding reception. It was a big hit.

1	small onion, chopped
¾	cup butter or margarine
2	cups Arborio or long grain rice
6	cups chicken broth
12	ounces fresh asparagus, cut into ½-inch pieces
12	ounces fontina cheese, shredded
1	cup grated Parmesan cheese

In a large saucepan cook chopped onion in butter till tender. Stir in rice. Add chicken broth and asparagus pieces. Bring to boiling.

Cook and stir over low heat till all of the liquid is evaporated. The rice is done when it is tender. (If necessary, add more broth during cooking.) Stir in fontina and Parmesan cheeses.

Makes 6 servings.

Radicchio Risotto

¾	cup butter or margarine
2	tablespoons olive oil
1	large onion, chopped
2	cups Arborio or long grain rice
6	cups water
1	pound radicchio, torn
½	cup dry white wine
½	teaspoon salt
½	teaspoon thread saffron, crushed
1	cup grated Parmesan cheese

Radicchio's bitter flavor is subdued when it's cooked with the rice. If you can't find radicchio, use arugula or chicory.

In a large saucepan melt butter over medium heat. Add oil. Add onion and cook until onion is tender. Stir in rice. Add water, radicchio, wine, salt, and saffron. Bring to boiling.

Cook and stir over low heat till all of the liquid is evaporated. The rice is done when it is tender. (If necessary, add more water during cooking.) Stir in Parmesan cheese.

Makes 6 servings.

Risotto with Apples

7	medium apples, sliced
1	cup butter or margarine
2	cups Arborio or long grain rice
6	cups water
¼	cup sugar
½	teaspoon cinnamon
½	teaspoon nutmeg
	Dash salt
1	cup grated Parmesan cheese

We like to serve this interesting risotto for Sunday brunch or with chicken and veal dishes.

In a large saucepan cook apples in butter till tender. Stir in rice. Add water, sugar, cinnamon, nutmeg, and salt. Bring to boiling.

Cook and stir over low heat till all of the liquid is evaporated. The rice is done when it is tender. (If necessary, add more water during cooking.) Stir in Parmesan cheese.

Makes 6 servings.

৪৪ Risotto with Peas and Pancetta ৯৯

Pancetta is referred to as Italian-style bacon. Unlike American bacon, which is cured in salt and smoked, pancetta is cured in salt and black pepper and is not smoked.

12 ounces pancetta or Canadian bacon, chopped
1 medium onion, chopped
½ cup butter or margarine
2 cups Arborio or long grain rice
6 cups chicken broth
½ teaspoon thread saffron, crushed
1 16-ounce can peas, drained
1 cup grated Parmesan cheese
Salt
Pepper

In a large saucepan cook pancetta or Canadian bacon and onion in butter till onion is tender. Stir in rice. Add chicken broth and saffron. Bring to boiling.

Cook and stir over low heat till all of the liquid is evaporated. The rice is done when it is tender. (If necessary, add more broth during cooking.) Stir in drained peas and Parmesan cheese; heat through. Season with salt and pepper.

Makes 6 servings.

VEGETABLES

My family would be lost without vegetables. We love the way they add texture and color to many of our recipes. But most of all, we love the way they taste. Give us a big serving of cooked vegetables and macaroni and we are very happy.

Since we think so highly of nature's harvest, most of our vegetable recipes are simple. This allows the subtle flavors to come through. Some of the simplest recipes are Asparagus and Pine Nuts, Sauteed Mushrooms, and Lorraine's Tomatoes. Other recipes, such as Vegetable Pie and Fresh Green Beans and Tomatoes, are a combination of vegetables, but just as easy to prepare.

Creamed Spinach

2	10-ounce packages frozen chopped spinach
1	small onion, chopped
2	tablespoons olive oil
2	3-ounce packages cream cheese
8	ounces mozzarella cheese, shredded (2 cups)
2	tablespoons grated Parmesan cheese
	Salt
	Pepper
	Garlic powder

My whole family goes absolutely crazy over this recipe. We eat creamed spinach every year at Thanksgiving and Christmas.

In a saucepan cook spinach according to package directions; drain. Meanwhile, in a large skillet cook onion in oil till tender. Stir in cooked spinach, cream, mozzarella and Parmesan cheeses. Season with salt, pepper, and garlic powder.

Transfer spinach mixture to a casserole dish. Bake, uncovered, in a 350°F oven about 20 minutes or till brown on top and heated through.

Makes 8 servings.

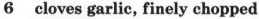

Fresh
Green Beans and Tomatoes

6	cloves garlic, finely chopped
¼	cup olive oil
2	16-ounce cans tomatoes
2	pounds fresh green beans, trimmed
¼	cup chopped parsley
	Salt
	Pepper

This goes well with roast beef or veal. If fresh green beans are not available, substitute three 9-ounce packages frozen whole or cut green beans.

In a large skillet cook garlic in oil till tender but not brown. Add tomatoes, green beans, and parsley. Bring to boiling; reduce heat. Cover and simmer about 30 minutes or till beans are tender. Season with salt and pepper.

Makes 8 servings.

Grandma's Baked Potatoes

Simple and delicious.

5   **medium potatoes, peeled and cubed**
¾   **cup olive oil**
½   **teaspoon salt**
½   **teaspoon pepper**
¼   **teaspoon dried oregano, crushed**
    Several dashes paprika

In a shallow baking pan toss together potatoes and oil. Sprinkle with salt, pepper, oregano, and paprika. Bake in a 475°F oven for 15 to 20 minutes or till potatoes are tender.

Makes 5 servings.

 ## Potatoes

Each variety of potato has its own characteristics. In general, round potatoes have firm, waxy meat that makes them best for boiling. Long, oval potatoes are mealy and best when baked, fried, or mashed.

When buying potatoes, choose those which are firm and smooth with shallow eyes. Avoid cut, sprouted, or blemished potatoes, and store them in a cool, dark place.

 ## Bianca's Fried Potatoes

Bianca, one of our cooks, is from central Italy, where many herbs and seasonings are used. She created this delicious potato dish with rosemary and pepper.

5   **medium potatoes, peeled and cubed**
1   **cup olive oil**
½   **teaspoon salt**
½   **teaspoon pepper**
    Dash ground red pepper
    Dash rosemary

In a large skillet fry potatoes in hot oil for 2 to 3 minutes or till golden brown. Drain on paper towels. Sprinkle with salt, pepper, red pepper, and rosemary.

Makes 5 servings.

Vegetable Pie

Butter or margarine
1   cup flavored bread crumbs
1   head cauliflower, cut into bite-size pieces
8   eggs, beaten
½   cup milk
½   cup grated Parmesan cheese
6   leaves fresh basil
3   cloves garlic, finely chopped
2   9-ounce packages frozen artichoke hearts, thawed

This resembles a quiche that is loaded with vegetables.

Butter the bottom and sides of a 10 × 9 × 2-inch baking dish or a deep 10-inch pie plate. Coat evenly with bread crumbs. Set aside. In a medium saucepan cook cauliflower in boiling water for 7 minutes or just till crisp-tender; drain.

In a mixing bowl stir together eggs, milk, ½ cup Parmesan cheese, basil, and garlic. Arrange artichoke hearts in the bottom of the prepared baking dish or pie plate. Pour the egg mixture over the artichoke hearts; arrange cauliflower pieces on top, and sprinkle with Parmesan cheese.

Bake in a 350°F oven for 20 minutes or till a knife inserted near the center comes out clean. Let the pie stand 5 minutes. Cut into wedges.

Makes 6 servings.

Lorraine's Tomatoes

2   medium tomatoes, halved crosswise
¼   cup olive oil
¼   cup dry bread crumbs
1   tablespoon chopped fresh basil or chervil

This wonderful, simple summer recipe is a gift to all of us from my Canadian friend, Lorraine.

In a medium skillet cook tomatoes, cut-side down, in hot oil for 1½ minutes. Turn and cook for 1½ minutes more. Remove from skillet. Add bread crumbs and basil or chervil to the skillet. Cook and stir till bread crumbs are toasted, then spoon bread crumb mixture on top of tomatoes.

Makes 4 servings.

Roasted Peppers

Eleanor (a special relative) makes these seasoned peppers with garlic, capers, and oregano.

6   medium green or red sweet peppers, cut into strips
2   tablespoons olive oil
3/4 cup dry bread crumbs
10 pitted ripe olives, chopped
3   cloves garlic, finely chopped
2   teaspoons capers
1/4 teaspoon dried oregano, crushed

In a shallow baking pan toss together peppers and oil. Sprinkle with bread crumbs, olives, garlic, capers, and dried oregano. Bake in 350°F oven for 1 hour or till peppers are tender, stirring once.

Makes 6 to 8 servings.

 Stuffed Artichokes

We eat these for our vegetable course, but they also make great appetizers.

6   medium artichokes
    Lemon juice
2   packages thin (Grissini) breadsticks, broken into pieces, or
1   cup dry bread crumbs
1/2 cup olive oil
1/4 cup chopped parsley
4   cloves garlic, finely chopped
5   fresh basil leaves, chopped, or 1/2 teaspoon dried basil, crushed
1/4 teaspoon salt
1/4 teaspoon pepper

Wash artichokes, trim stems, and remove any loose outer leaves. Cut 1-inch off the tops. Snip off any sharp leaf tips. Brush cut edges of leaves with lemon juice to prevent browning.

In a dutch oven cook artichokes in boiling water about 25 minutes or till a leaf pulls out easily. Remove artichokes with a slotted spoon and invert on paper towels to drain.

Meanwhile, in a mixing bowl stir together bread crumbs, oil, parsley, garlic, basil, salt, and pepper.

Place artichokes in shallow baking pan. Spoon bread crumb mixture between the leaves. Bake in a 350°F oven for 30 minutes or till bread mixture is brown. To eat, pull off one leaf at a time and eat with bread crumb mixture. Spoon out and discard the fuzzy choke and eat the artichoke heart.

Makes 6 servings.

 ## Asparagus and Pine Nuts

1 pound asparagus, trimmed, or 1 10-ounce package frozen asparagus spears
5 cloves garlic, finely chopped
2 tablespoons pine nuts or chopped walnuts
2 tablespoons olive oil
 Salt
 Pepper

This is enormously popular at our store when fresh asparagus is in season.

Cook asparagus in boiling water for 10 minutes or till crisp-tender. Drain. Meanwhile, in a small skillet cook garlic and nuts in oil till garlic is tender and nuts are light brown. Pour over asparagus. Season with salt and pepper.

Makes 4 servings.

 ## Asparagus

When buying asparagus, choose firm, straight stalks that have closed tips. Avoid asparagus with wilted stalks or loose tips. To store, wrap the stems in damp paper towels and refrigerate in a plastic bag. Use within 1 or 2 days.

To prepare asparagus for cooking, take each spear and bend the stem end gently in half. It will snap, separating the woody end and the tender stalk. Discard the ends. Cook the stalks according to the recipe or steam about 8 minutes or till crisp-tender.

Sauteed Mushrooms

1 pound fresh mushrooms, sliced
1 large onion, sliced
¼ cup olive oil
Salt
Pepper
2 tablespoons chopped parsley

In a large skillet cook sliced mushrooms and onion in oil till tender. Season with salt and pepper. Sprinkle with chopped parsley.

Makes 4 servings.

 Fried Gardunias

A gardunia is a winter vegetable that looks like an enormous stalk of celery and tastes like a cross between celery and licorice. It is usually available from October to January.

1 medium stalk gardunia, cut into 2-inch pieces
3 eggs
½ cup milk
¼ teaspoon garlic powder
¼ teaspoon salt
⅛ teaspoon pepper
2 cups dry bread crumbs
1 to 2 cups olive oil

In a large saucepan cook gardunia in boiling water for 2 hours or till tender. Drain. In a mixing bowl stir together eggs, milk, garlic powder, salt, and pepper. Dip gardunias in egg mixture. Coat with bread crumbs. Dip again in egg mixture.

Fry gardunias in hot oil for 2 minutes per side or till golden brown. Drain on paper towels.

Makes 8 to 10 servings.

Fried Zucchini Flowers

1   egg
8   ounces ricotta cheese
8   ounces mozzarella cheese, shredded (2 cups)
24 zucchini flowers
1   egg, beaten
½   cup flour
½   cup olive oil

These cheese-stuffed blossoms are Grandma D'Angelo's specialty.

In a mixing bowl combine egg with both cheeses. Mix well. Gently spoon egg-cheese mixture into the center of each flower. Dip flower in beaten egg; coat with flour.

Fry zucchini flowers in hot oil for 1 to 2 minutes or till golden brown. Drain on paper towels.

Makes 12 servings.

Baked Apples and Yams

4   medium apples, peeled and sliced
4   medium yams or sweet potatoes, peeled and sliced
2   medium onions, sliced
½   cup butter or margarine
½   cup packed brown sugar

This is one of our favorite Thanksgiving vegetable recipes.

In a shallow baking pan layer half the sliced applies, yams, and onions. Dot with half the butter. Sprinkle with half the brown sugar. Repeat layering of the remaining apples, yams, and onions.

Dot with remaining butter; sprinkle with remaining brown sugar. Bake in a 350°F oven about 1 hour or till tender.

Makes 6 servings.

Baked Peppers

This dish is so easy, and so good!

5   **medium green or red sweet peppers, cut into strips**
¼   **cup olive oil**
1   **teaspoon salt**

In a shallow baking pan toss together peppers and oil. Sprinkle with salt. Bake in a 350°F oven for 45 minutes or till peppers are tender, stirring occasionally.

Makes 6 servings.

FRITTATAS

Frittatas are often referred to as Italian omelets. Unlike French omelets, which are cooked quickly and folded, frittatas are cooked slowly and are served open.

The basis of all frittatas is a mixture of eggs, milk, hard grated cheese, salt, and pepper. Then you can add almost anything you like. Vegetables, meats, cheeses, and even fruit can enhance the flavor and texture of the basic egg mixture. Choose your favorite foods or try the flavor combinations in the recipes that follow.

Making a perfect frittata may take a little practice. For best results, be sure the bottom of your skillet is covered with oil. Without enough oil, your frittata may stick and be difficult to flip. If you're using a teflon-coated pan, you can use less oil.

We usually serve frittatas for dinner in warm weather, accompanied by salad and bread. For an exceptional brunch for six people, any of the recipes can be doubled and prepared in a large 12-inch skillet.

Mozzarella-Spinach-Bacon Frittata

6   **eggs**
½   **cup milk**
3   **tablespoons grated Parmesan cheese**
    Salt
    Pepper
    Oregano, basil, or parsley (optional)
2   **tablespoons olive oil**
6   **ounces fresh mozzarella cheese, chopped**
1   **cup fresh spinach or ½ of a 10-ounce package frozen chopped spinach, thawed and drained**
4   **slices bacon, cooked crisp and crumbled**

The combination of flavors in this recipe is extraordinary! It's by far my favorite frittata.

In a large bowl beat eggs. Add milk, Parmesan cheese, salt, and pepper. Add oregano, basil, or parsley, if desired. Mix well.

In an 8-inch skillet heat oil over medium-low heat. Add egg mixture. As eggs set, run a spatula around edge of the skillet. Lift the eggs to allow the uncooked portion to flow underneath.

Arrange mozzarella cheese over egg mixture. Top with spinach and bacon. Cover skillet and cook for 2 minutes. Uncover. Carefully lift eggs with a spatula and flip. (Or slide frittata out of skillet onto a pie plate or plate. Invert egg mixture into skillet.) Cook for about 2 minutes more.

Makes 2 or 3 servings.

❧ Tomato-Basil-Parmesan Frittata ❧

*There is no substitute for
fresh basil in this classic
Italian frittata.*

6   **eggs**
½   **cup milk**
3   **tablespoons grated Parmesan cheese**
    Salt
    Pepper
2   **tablespoons olive oil**
1   **tomato, sliced**
6   **fresh basil leaves**
6   **ounces Parmesan cheese, cut into chunks**

In a large bowl beat eggs. Add milk, 3 tablespoons cheese, salt,
and pepper. Mix well.

In an 8-inch skillet heat oil over medium-low heat. Add egg
mixture. As eggs set, run a spatula around edge of the skillet. Lift the eggs to allow the uncooked portion to flow underneath.

Arrange tomato over egg mixture. Top with basil and 6
ounces Parmesan cheese. Cover skillet and cook for 2 minutes. Uncover. Carefully lift eggs with a spatula and flip. (Or
slide frittata out of skillet onto a pie plate or plate. Invert egg
mixture into skillet.) Cook for about 2 minutes more.

Makes 2 or 3 servings.

❧ Shrimp and Bacon Frittata ❧

*This is equally superb
with 4 to 6 ounces of
cooked crab instead of
the shrimp.*

6   **eggs**
½   **cup milk**
3   **tablespoons grated Parmesan cheese**
    Salt
    Pepper
    Oregano, basil, or parsley (optional)
2   **tablespoons olive oil**
4   **ounces small cooked shrimp**
4   **slices bacon, cooked crisp and crumbled**

In a large bowl beat eggs. Add milk, Parmesan cheese, salt,
and pepper. Add oregano, basil, or parsley, if desired. Mix
well.

In an 8-inch skillet heat oil over medium-low heat. Add egg mixture. As eggs set, run a spatula around edge of the skillet. Lift the eggs to allow the uncooked portion to flow underneath.

Arrange shrimp over egg mixture. Sprinkle with bacon. Cover skillet and cook for 2 minutes. Uncover. Carefully lift eggs with a spatula and flip. (Or slide frittata out of skillet onto a pie plate or plate. Invert egg mixture into skillet.) Cook for about 2 minutes more.

Makes 2 or 3 servings.

 ## Frittata Primavera

6	eggs
½	cup milk
3	tablespoons grated Parmesan cheese
	Salt
	Pepper
	Oregano, basil, or parsley (optional)
1 ½	cups chopped fresh vegetables (broccoli, zucchini, mushrooms, or onion)
2	tablespoons olive oil

Use your favorite medley of vegetables for this colorful frittata. In a hurry? Save time by using frozen, thawed vegetables instead of fresh ones.

In a large bowl beat eggs. Add milk, Parmesan cheese, salt, and pepper. Add oregano, basil, or parsley, if desired. Mix well.

In a small saucepan steam vegetables till crisp-tender. Drain and set aside. In an 8-inch skillet heat oil over medium-low heat. Add egg mixture. As eggs set, run a spatula around edge of the skillet. Lift the eggs to allow the uncooked portion to flow underneath.

Spoon vegetable mixture over eggs. Cover skillet and cook for 2 minutes. Uncover. Carefully lift eggs with a spatula and flip. (Or slide frittata out of skillet onto a pie plate or plate. Invert egg mixture into skillet.) Cook for about 2 minutes more.

Makes 2 or 3 servings.

Finocchi Frittata

Finocchi is the Italian word for fennel. We use fresh, cooked fennel to give this frittata its unique flavor.

6   **eggs**
½   **cup milk**
3   **tablespoons grated Parmesan cheese**
   Salt
   Pepper
   Oregano, basil, or parsley (optional)
2   **tablespoons olive oil**
1   **tomato, sliced**
½   **of a small head radicchio, thinly sliced**
½   **fresh fennel bulb, sliced and steamed**

In a large bowl beat eggs. Add milk, Parmesan cheese, salt, and pepper. Add oregano, basil, or parsley, if desired. Mix well.

In an 8-inch skillet heat oil over medium-low heat. Add egg mixture. As eggs set, run a spatula around edge of the skillet. Lift the eggs to allow the uncooked portion to flow underneath.

Arrange tomato over egg mixture. Top with radicchio and fennel. Cover skillet and cook for 2 minutes. Uncover. Carefully lift eggs with a spatula and flip. (Or slide frittata out of skillet onto a pie plate or plate. Invert egg mixture into skillet.) Cook for about 2 minutes more.

Makes 2 or 3 servings.

In an 8-inch skillet heat oil over medium-low heat. Add egg mixture. As eggs set, run a spatula around edge of the skillet. Lift the eggs to allow the uncooked portion to flow underneath.

Arrange shrimp over egg mixture. Sprinkle with bacon. Cover skillet and cook for 2 minutes. Uncover. Carefully lift eggs with a spatula and flip. (Or slide frittata out of skillet onto a pie plate or plate. Invert egg mixture into skillet.) Cook for about 2 minutes more.

Makes 2 or 3 servings.

 ## Frittata Primavera

6   eggs
½   cup milk
3   tablespoons grated Parmesan cheese
     Salt
     Pepper
     Oregano, basil, or parsley (optional)
1 ½ cups chopped fresh vegetables (broccoli,
     zucchini, mushrooms, or onion)
2   tablespoons olive oil

Use your favorite medley of vegetables for this colorful frittata. In a hurry? Save time by using frozen, thawed vegetables instead of fresh ones.

In a large bowl beat eggs. Add milk, Parmesan cheese, salt, and pepper. Add oregano, basil, or parsley, if desired. Mix well.

In a small saucepan steam vegetables till crisp-tender. Drain and set aside. In an 8-inch skillet heat oil over medium-low heat. Add egg mixture. As eggs set, run a spatula around edge of the skillet. Lift the eggs to allow the uncooked portion to flow underneath.

Spoon vegetable mixture over eggs. Cover skillet and cook for 2 minutes. Uncover. Carefully lift eggs with a spatula and flip. (Or slide frittata out of skillet onto a pie plate or plate. Invert egg mixture into skillet.) Cook for about 2 minutes more.

Makes 2 or 3 servings.

Finocchi Frittata

Finocchi is the Italian word for fennel. We use fresh, cooked fennel to give this frittata its unique flavor.

6 eggs
½ cup milk
3 tablespoons grated Parmesan cheese
   Salt
   Pepper
   Oregano, basil, or parsley (optional)
2 tablespoons olive oil
1 tomato, sliced
½ of a small head radicchio, thinly sliced
½ fresh fennel bulb, sliced and steamed

In a large bowl beat eggs. Add milk, Parmesan cheese, salt, and pepper. Add oregano, basil, or parsley, if desired. Mix well.

In an 8-inch skillet heat oil over medium-low heat. Add egg mixture. As eggs set, run a spatula around edge of the skillet. Lift the eggs to allow the uncooked portion to flow underneath.

Arrange tomato over egg mixture. Top with radicchio and fennel. Cover skillet and cook for 2 minutes. Uncover. Carefully lift eggs with a spatula and flip. (Or slide frittata out of skillet onto a pie plate or plate. Invert egg mixture into skillet.) Cook for about 2 minutes more.

Makes 2 or 3 servings.

DESSERTS

N o matter how plentiful our main course is, we always serve dessert. It's an essential part of the meal because it gives us a chance to linger at the dinner table.

Many of the recipes in this chapter can be made in advance, especially the cookies and cakes. But when time is at a premium and even the make-ahead recipes don't fit your schedule, you can always prepare one of our favorite and easiest desserts: cheese and fruit. The four cheeses we serve year-round are provolone, fontina, gorgonzola, and mascarpone. In the winter, we add such fruits as apples, grapes, bananas, persimmons, and pomegranates. In the summer, we choose assorted berries, plums, peaches, nectarines, and melons. We simply arrange the fruits and cheeses on a serving platter and let everyone help themselves.

At our house, dessert wouldn't be complete without a cup of steaming coffee. Brew 4 cups espresso or strong coffee. Meanwhile, in a heavy saucepan heat 2 cups milk and ¼ cup sugar. Add espresso to saucepan. Simmer for 4 minutes. Serve in large coffee cups. Makes 4 satisfying servings.

Melon Soup

1 medium cantaloupe
1 cup orange juice
⅓ cup heavy cream
¼ cup cream sherry
Fresh mint (optional)

This is a perfect, light summer dessert or first course. My sister Nina makes this for us.

Cut cantaloupe in half and remove the seeds. Scoop out cantaloupe pulp. In a blender container or food processor bowl, combine cantaloupe pulp, orange juice, cream, and sherry. Cover and blend till smooth.

To make each melon half rest firmly on a plate, trim a thin slice from the bottom. Pour blended melon mixture into melon halves. Garnish with fresh mint, if desired.

Makes 2 servings.

Nina's Baked Walnut Pears

3 medium pears
2 tablespoons flour
2 tablespoons brown sugar
2 tablespoons butter or margarine, softened
½ cup chopped walnuts
Ouo-Miel (Italian egg and honey liqueur) or orange liqueur

Choose pears that are ripe but still firm so they will hold their shape during baking.

Halve pears and remove cores. In a mixing bowl, stir together flour and brown sugar. Cut in butter till mixture is crumbly. Stir in walnuts.

Place pears, cut side up, on a baking sheet. Sprinkle with liqueur. Spoon walnut mixture into the center of each pear. Sprinkle with more liqueur, if desired.

Bake in a 350°F oven for 10 minutes or till pears are tender, then broil pears for 2 minutes or till walnut mixture is brown and crisp. Serve warm or at room temperature.

Makes 6 servings.

Rice Pudding

We adore this pudding! Our friend Ron perfected the recipe and agreed we could share it with you.

6   cups milk
1   cup long grain rice
1   egg
1   cup sugar
¾   cup heavy cream

In a large, heavy saucepan bring milk and rice to boiling. Reduce heat. Cover and simmer for 30 to 40 minutes or till rice is tender and most of the milk is absorbed. Stir occasionally during cooking.

Meanwhile, stir together egg, sugar, and cream. Add to cooked rice mixture. Stir till well combined. For added creaminess, mix in one pint vanilla ice cream just before serving.

Makes 10 servings.

 # Pumpkin Pie

This is no ordinary pumpkin pie. Ricotta cheese distinguishes the Manganaro version of this Thanksgiving favorite.

2   cups flour
1   tablespoon sugar
5   tablespoons shortening
5   tablespoons butter or margarine
6 to 8   tablespoons cold water
1½   cups cooked, mashed pumpkin or one
         16-ounce can pumpkin
1   cup brown sugar
1   teaspoon ground cinnamon
½   teaspoon ground ginger
⅛   teaspoon salt
2   eggs
1   pound ricotta cheese

In a mixing bowl stir together flour and sugar. Cut in shortening and butter till pieces are the size of small peas. Sprinkle 1 tablespoon of the water over part of the mixture; gently toss with a fork. Push to side of bowl. Repeat till all is moistened. Form dough into 2 balls. Wrap in clear plastic wrap and chill for 30 minutes.

On a lightly floured surface, flatten one ball of dough with hands. Roll dough from center to edge, forming a circle about 12 inches in diameter. Ease pastry into a 9-inch pie plate, being careful not to stretch pastry. Trim pastry to ½ inch beyond edge of pie plate. Roll out remaining pastry. Cut into ½-inch-wide strips.

In a mixing bowl stir together pumpkin, brown sugar, cinnamon, ginger, and salt. In another bowl combine eggs and ricotta cheese. Fold into pumpkin mixture. Pour into pastry-lined pie plate.

Weave pastry strips over filling to make a lattice crust. Press ends of strips into rim of crust. Fold bottom pastry over the lattice strips; seal and flute.

Bake in a 350°F oven for 30 minutes or till crust is golden brown and a knife inserted near the center comes out clean.

Makes 8 servings.

 ## Honey Balls

4 cups flour
1 teaspoon baking powder
 Dash salt
6 eggs, beaten
2 cups cooking oil
 Honey
 Small multicolored candies (optional)

Our grandmother serves these fried pastries piled up on plates to resemble beehives.

In a mixing bowl stir together flour, baking powder, and salt. Add eggs and stir till smooth. Roll dough into 1-inch balls. Fry in hot oil for 2 to 3 minutes or till golden brown. Drain on paper towels.

Pile honey balls on 2 plates to look like beehives. In a double boiler heat honey over low heat. Drizzle honey over the "hives." Sprinkle with multicolored candies, if desired.

Makes 3 to 5 dozen honey balls.

Honey Bows

Serve these alongside a large scoop of ice cream or sorbet.

1   cup flour
    Dash salt
2   eggs
2   cups cooking oil
    Warm honey or powdered sugar

In a mixing bowl combine flour and salt. Add eggs and stir till well combined. On a lightly floured surface roll dough to ¼-inch thickness. Cut into strips. Fry in hot oil for 1 to 2 minutes or till golden brown. Drain on paper towels. Drizzle with honey or sprinkle with powdered sugar.

Makes 12 to 16 servings.

Chocolate-Dipped Acorn Cookies

We eat these tasty nuggets by the handful.

1   cup butter or margarine
⅔   cup sugar
3   egg yolks
1   teaspoon almond extract
2½   cups flour
2 or 3 drops green food coloring
5   ounces (5 squares) semisweet chocolate, melted

In a mixing bowl beat butter till smooth. Add sugar and beat till light and fluffy. Add egg yolks and almond extract; beat till well combined. Gradually add flour, beating till well combined. Add green food coloring; beat till well combined.

Using about 1 teaspoon dough for each cookie, shape into balls that resemble acorns (pointed at one end). Place on an ungreased cookie sheet.

Bake in a 375°F oven about 10 minutes or till done. Cool on a wire rack. When cool, dip one end of each cookie in melted chocolate. Place on waxed paper to dry. Chill.

Makes about 50 cookies.

Pastiera di Grana
(Wheat Berry-Ricotta Pie)

½	cup wheat berries
1½	cups water
2	cups flour
1	tablespoon sugar
5	tablespoons shortening
5	tablespoons butter or margarine
6 to 8	tablespoons cold water
12	ounces ricotta cheese
1	cup sugar
2	eggs
2	teaspoons orange flower water
1	teaspoon lemon juice
½	teaspoon lemon extract
½	pound candied citron, diced

Wheat berries (unpolished whole wheat kernels) give this pie a unique texture. You can purchase wheat berries at most health food stores. Both of my grandmothers made this heavenly pie.

Soak wheat berries in 1½ cups water in the refrigerator overnight. Transfer berries and water to a saucepan. Bring to boiling; reduce heat. Cover and simmer for 30 minutes or till berries are tender. Cool.

For the pastry, in a mixing bowl stir together flour and sugar. Cut in shortening and butter till pieces are the size of small peas. Sprinkle 1 tablespoon of the water over part of the mixture; gently toss with a fork. Push to side of bowl. Repeat till all is moistened. Form dough into 2 balls. Wrap in clear plastic wrap and chill for 30 minutes.

On a lightly floured surface, flatten one ball of dough with hands. Roll dough from center to edge, forming a circle about 12 inches in diameter. Ease pastry into a 9-inch pie plate, being careful not to stretch pastry. Trim pastry to ½ inch beyond edge of pie plate. Roll out remaining pastry. Cut into ½-inch-wide strips.

In a mixing bowl combine cooked wheat berries, ricotta cheese, sugar, eggs, flower water, lemon juice, lemon extract, and citron. Stir till well combined. Spoon into pie shell. Weave pastry strips over filling to make a lattice crust. Press ends of strips into rim of crust. Fold bottom pastry over the lattice strips; seal and flute. Bake in a 350°F oven for 30 minutes or till pastry is golden brown.

Makes 8 servings.

Cream Cheese Pound Cake

¾ cup butter or margarine
1 8-ounce package cream cheese
2 teaspoons vanilla
2 cups sugar
5 eggs
3 cups flour
3 ½ teaspoons baking powder
½ teaspoon salt
⅔ cup milk

In a mixing bowl beat butter, cream cheese, and vanilla till smooth. Add sugar and beat till light and fluffy. Add eggs, one at a time, beating 1 to 2 minutes after each. Scrape bowl frequently.

In another mixing bowl stir together flour, baking powder, and salt. Add flour mixture and milk alternately to beaten mixture, beating well after each addition.

Generously grease a 10-inch tube pan. Line the bottom with waxed paper. Pour cake batter into prepared pan. Bake in a 350°F oven about 1 hour or till a toothpick inserted near the center comes out clean. Cool in the pan on a wire rack for 10 minutes. Remove cake from pan and place on wire rack; remove waxed paper and leave on wire rack to cool thoroughly.

Makes 12 servings.

Almond Cookies

These cookies are so simple and so good! We like to make them for the holidays and package them in festive tins for friends. The recipe comes from my grandmother D'Angelo.

2 cups butter or margarine
½ cup sugar
1 teaspoon vanilla
4 cups sifted flour
2 cups finely chopped almonds
Sugar

In a large mixing bowl beat butter till smooth. Add sugar and beat till light and fluffy. Beat in vanilla. Gradually add flour, beating till well combined. Stir in almonds.

On a lightly floured surface roll dough ½ inch thick. Use a sharp knife to cut dough into 1½ inch pieces. Place on an ungreased cookie sheet.

Bake in a 350°F oven for 10 to 12 minutes or till edges are firm and bottoms are light brown. Roll in sugar while warm. Cool on wire racks.

Makes 4 to 6 dozen cookies.

Pasqua (Easter) Chocolate Cheesecake

2	8-ounce packages cream cheese
1	cup sugar
8	ounces ricotta cheese
1	tablespoon vanilla
5	eggs
1	cup semisweet chocolate pieces
1	tablespoon lemon juice
4	ounces ricotta cheese
¼	cup sugar
¼	cup butter or margarine, softened
	Unsweetened cocoa powder (optional)

Yes, it's as sinfully rich as it sounds!

In a mixing bowl beat cream cheese till smooth. Add 1 cup sugar, 8 ounces ricotta cheese, and vanilla. Beat till well combined. Add eggs all at once. Beat just till combined (do not overbeat). Divide mixture in half. Fold semisweet chocolate pieces into half of the beaten mixture; stir lemon juice into the other half.

Pour the lemon mixture into a well-buttered 9-inch springform pan. Spread the chocolate mixture on top. Bake in a 350°F oven for 40 to 45 minutes or till the center appears to be set; cool for 10 minutes.

Meanwhile, in a mixing bowl beat 4 ounces ricotta cheese, ¼ cup sugar, and butter till well combined. Spread over cheesecake. Loosen sides of cheesecake from pan; remove sides of pan. Sprinkle with cocoa powder, if desired.

Makes 12 servings.

Fig Bars

Another special treat from my grandmother. She makes a huge holiday batch of these bars so we can all take some home.

1	**pound dried figs**
1	**pound pitted whole dates**
1	**cup raisins**
½	**cup walnuts**
1	**3 ½-ounce package candied lemon citron, diced**
1	**3 ½-ounce package candied orange citron, diced**
1	**3-ounce package candied cherries, diced**
2	**tablespoons orange extract**
2	**tablespoons lemon extract**
1	**cup honey**
2 ½	**cups sifted flour**
1	**teaspoon baking powder**
	Dash salt
1	**cup butter or margarine**
¾	**cup sugar**
2	**eggs**
1	**teaspoon vanilla**

For filling, place figs, dates, raisins, and walnuts in a food processor. Cover and process till well combined. (Or finely chop or grind figs, dates, raisins, and walnuts.) Stir in lemon and orange citron, cherries, orange and lemon extracts. Add honey; stir till well combined.

For dough, in a mixing bowl stir together flour, baking powder, and salt. In another mixing bowl beat butter till smooth. Add sugar and beat till fluffy. Add egg and vanilla and beat till well combined. Gradually add flour mixture, beating till well combined.

On a lightly floured surface roll dough ¼-inch thick. Cut into 3 × 2-inch rectangles. Place half of the rectangles 1 inch apart on ungreased cookie sheets. Spoon about 1 rounded tablespoon filling onto each rectangle. Top with remaining rectangles. Seal edges. Bake in a 375°F oven for 12 to 15 minutes or till edges are firm and bottoms are lightly browned. Remove from cookie sheets and cool on wire racks.

Makes about 24 fig bars.

Nina's Vanilla Cream Puffs

½   cup shortening
1   cup water
1   cup flour
2   teaspoons baking powder
⅛   teaspoon salt
3   eggs
½   cup sugar
2   tablespoons cornstarch
⅛   teaspoon salt
1   cup milk
2   egg yolks
1   tablespoon butter or margarine
1   teaspoon vanilla

Try this recipe when company is coming. You can make the cream puffs and vanilla filling in advance.

For cream puffs, in a saucepan melt shortening. Add water; bring to boiling. Stir together flour, baking powder, and ⅛ teaspoon salt. Add to boiling mixture all at once. Stir vigorously. Cook and stir till mixture forms a ball that doesn't separate.

Remove from heat. Cool slightly, about 5 minutes. Add eggs, one at a time, beating vigorously with a wooden spoon after each addition. Drop by heaping tablespoonfuls, 3 inches apart, on a greased baking sheet. Bake in a 400°F oven for 25 to 30 minutes or till golden brown and puffy. Remove from oven; split open. Remove any soft dough inside. Cool on a wire rack.

For filling, in a heavy medium saucepan combine sugar, cornstarch, and ⅛ teaspoon salt. Stir in milk. Cook and stir over medium heat till thickened and bubbly. Cook and stir 2 minutes more. Remove from heat. Gradually stir about 1 cup hot mixture into egg yolks. Return all of the mixture to saucepan. Cook and stir 2 minutes more. Remove from heat. Stir in butter and vanilla till butter melts. Pour into a bowl. Cover surface with clear plastic wrap. Chill without stirring.

To assemble, spoon vanilla filling into cooled puffs.

Makes about 10 cream puffs.

❧ Starlight Double Delight Cake ❧

We find this cake a double delight because the chocolate mixture doubles as the cake batter and the frosting.

1	8-ounce package cream cheese
½	cup shortening
1	pound sifted powdered sugar (about 4¾ cups)
½	teaspoon vanilla
¼	cup hot water
4	ounces (4 squares) semisweet chocolate, melted
¼	cup shortening
3	eggs
2¼	cups flour
1½	teaspoons baking soda
1	teaspoon salt
¾	cup milk

In a mixing bowl beat cream cheese and ½ cup shortening till smooth. Add half the sugar and the vanilla and beat till light and fluffy. Add remaining sugar and hot water alternately to cream cheese mixture, beating well after each addition. Add chocolate; beat till well combined. Divide mixture in half.

To half of the chocolate mixture add ¼ cup shortening; beat till well combined. Add eggs, one at a time, beating 1 to 2 minutes after each.

Stir together flour, baking soda, and salt. Add flour mixture and milk alternately to beaten mixture, beating well after each addition. Grease and lightly flour two 9 × 1½-inch round baking pans. Pour cake batter into pans.

Bake in a 350°F oven for 30 to 35 minutes or till a toothpick inserted near the center comes out clean. Cool 10 minutes on wire racks. Remove from pans. Cool thoroughly. Frost cooled cake with remaining chocolate mixture.

Makes 12 servings.

Vanilla Cheesecake

2 ½ cups graham cracker crumbs
¼   cup sugar
¼   cup butter or margarine, melted
3   8-ounce packages cream cheese
1   cup sugar
5   eggs
1   teaspoon vanilla
2   cups sour cream
½   cup sugar
1   teaspoon vanilla
     Fruit (optional)

This cream cheese and sour cream indulgence will melt in your mouth.

In a mixing bowl stir together graham cracker crumbs and ¼ cup sugar. Add melted butter, stirring till well combined. Press graham cracker crumb mixture in the bottom and up the sides of a 13 × 9 × 2-inch baking pan. Chill.

In another mixing bowl beat cream cheese till smooth. Add 1 cup sugar and beat till light and fluffy. Add eggs and 1 teaspoon vanilla; beat till just combined. Pour beaten mixture into graham cracker crust.

Bake in a 300°F oven for 1 hour or till a knife inserted near the center comes out clean. Stir together sour cream, ½ cup sugar, and 1 teaspoon vanilla. Spread over top of cheesecake. Bake for 5 minutes more. Cool on wire rack. Serve with fruit, if desired.

Makes 12 servings.

THE ITALIAN GROCER

Are you wondering what mascarpone is? Are you puzzled about prosciutto? To help answer these questions and many more, we've included this special section. We've explained the fundamentals of olive oils, Italian cheeses, Italian meats, and of course, pasta. We've included buying and storing information in addition to flavor comments. And don't ignore the handy pasta cooking chart we've added at the end.

As we've said before, our recipes are simple as well as delicious. We hope this chapter helps you enjoy trying every one.

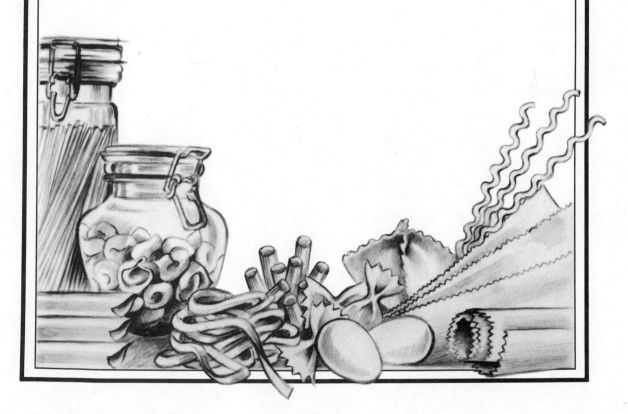

OLIVE OILS

*L*ike most Italian cooks, we use olive oil liberally. It is a critical ingredient in much of the cooking we do at the store and at home.

Olive oil is produced in Italy, Spain, Greece, France, and California. According to an old Tuscan saying, "Where there's good wine, there's good oil." Many areas in Italy produce good wines—and good olive oils.

The color of olive oil can vary from golden to green and the flavor can range from fruity to mellow to peppery.

Types of Olive Oils

In Italy, the different types of olive oils are designated by law. The classification of each oil depends upon its level of acidity. The less acidity, the better the oil.*

Extra virgin olive oil, considered to be the best, is made from the first cold pressing of the olives. It is produced from olives that have been mechanically crushed and have not been chemically treated. The finest extra virgin oils tend to be made by hand. By law, this oil cannot contain more than 1 percent of oleic acid.

Superfine virgin olive oil is made just like extra virgin oil, but the acidity is allowed to reach 1.5 percent.

Fine virgin olive oil has an acidity greater than 1.5 percent and less than 3.0 percent. It is made from oils extracted by treating the previously pressed olive pulp with solvents.

Pure virgin olive oil contains acidity greater than 3.0 percent and less than 4.0 percent. It is also made from oils extracted by treating the previously pressed olive pulp with solvents.

Pure olive oil is made like pure virgin olive oil and has acidity that exceeds 4.0 percent.

*U.S. labeling regulations are less strict than Italian laws when it comes to olive oil. They specify only that oil labeled "virgin" must come from the first pressing of the olives. There is no U.S. specification for extra virgin olive oil.

The Italian Grocer

Storing Olive Oil —————————————————

We never have trouble using our supply of olive oil. In fact, it seems that we never have enough! But for those of you who don't use it so often, here are some storage tips to keep in mind.

◦§ Olive oil, unlike some wine, does not improve with age. Since it has not been heat-treated or preserved, olive oil can become bitter-tasting and rancid.

◦§ Store olive oil at room temperature for 1 to 2 months.

◦§ For longer storage, keep olive oil in your refrigerator. The oil will turn cloudy and coagulate, but it will clear when set at room temperature. You can store olive oil in your refrigerator for 1 to 2 years.

ITALIAN MEATS

Cappicola

Cappicola is a boneless pork shoulder butt that is seasoned with ground hot or sweet peppers, paprika, salt, and sugar. It is mildly cured and air-dried.

Mortadella

Mortadella is a semi-dry sausage from Bologna, Italy. It is made from many cuts of pork that are finely ground and seasoned with garlic and anise. Mortadella has a smooth texture and is smoked at a high temperature and air-dried.

Pancetta

Pancetta is also called Italian bacon because it is from the pork belly but it is not smoked, like American bacon. It is dry salt-cured with other spices and rolled up in a salami shape.

Pepperoni

Pepperoni is a dry sausage of coarsely cut beef and pork. It is seasoned with a variety of spices including ground red pepper.

Prosciutto

Prosciutto is a salted and air-cured Italian ham. There are different forms of prosciutto.

Prosciutto fresco is raw ham used in cooking.

Prosciutto crudo is cured ham made from salted hind hams. It is cured in fresh, dry air for as long as 1½ years. It is not smoked. It has a pink or pale red color and is ringed with fat. Do not trim the fat before cooking or you will lose some of the flavor.

Prosciutto cotto is boiled or baked ham. It is not smoked and comes from the pig's hind. Look for prosciutto cotto that is fleshy and pink.

Salami, Calabrese

Calabrese salami is a dry sausage made from all pork and seasoned with hot peppers.

Salami, Cotto

Cotto salami can be cooked or smoked and is seasoned with peppercorns.

Salami, Easter Nola

Easter Nola salami is a dry sausage of coarsely chopped pork, mildly seasoned with black pepper and garlic.

Salami, Genoa

Genoa salami is a dry sausage usually made entirely of pork, but it may contain a small amount of beef. It is moistened with wine or grape juice and seasoned with garlic.

Salami, Milano

Milano salami is a dry salami that is made from pork and finely cut beef. It is spiced with garlic.

Salsiccia

Salsiccia is a highly seasoned fresh sausage made from finely chopped pork.

ITALIC CHEESES

All the cheeses used in our recipes are imported from Italy. Although good domestic cheeses are available today, we are most familiar with imported cheeses. Here is a rundown on the cheeses we prefer.

Asiago

Asiago is a sharp-flavored, light yellow cheese. It is round and flat and may be coated with paraffin. It has a semisoft texture when cured for 60 days, a medium texture when cured for 6 months, and a hard texture when cured for 12 months.

To store asiago, wrap in aluminum foil or good quality plastic wrap. Store in the refrigerator for several weeks for semisoft cheese or several months for hard cheese.

Fontina

Fontina in Italy is made from ewe's milk and can range in flavor from delicate and nutty to robust and salty. It is a semisoft to hard cheese and usually comes in a wheel shape with tiny holes on its surface.

To store fontina, wrap it in aluminum foil or good quality plastic wrap. Store in the refrigerator for a few weeks.

Gorgonzola

Gorgonzola is a blue-veined cheese with a strong, pungent flavor and aroma. It tastes somewhat like blue cheese but is less salty.

To store gorgonzola, wrap it in aluminum foil or good quality plastic wrap. Store in the refrigerator for a few weeks.

Mascarpone

This is a rich, thick, velvety cheese that resembles clotted cream. It has a very high butterfat content which makes it especially good for desserts.

Store mascarpone in the refrigerator in a covered container for 1 week.

Mozzarella

Mozzarella has a mild and delicate flavor that makes it a good choice for many recipes. It has a semisoft, plastic-like consistency and smooth texture that gets stringy when heated. It is a creamy white color and comes in a variety of shapes and sizes. Mozzarella is available cured or uncured and is made with whole or lowfat milk.

To store mozzarella, wrap in aluminum foil or good quality plastic wrap. Store in the refrigerator for several weeks.

Parmesan

The best imported cheese in this category is Parmigiano-Reggiano, which is produced in Emilia-Romagna. Any cheese produced outside of this zone cannot be called Parmigiano-Reggiano. The strict codes governing this cheese-producing area specify that no additives can be introduced during the cheese-making. It is simply made with cows milk and rennet and aged for a minimum of 2 years.

Parmesan is a hard, granular cheese and is usually grated before serving. It has a sharp flavor that compliments many Italian foods.

To store Parmesan, wrap each piece in aluminum foil or good quality plastic wrap. Store in the refrigerator for several months.

Provolone

This cheese varies from mild to sharp and has a slightly smoky flavor. It is a light golden cheese with a firm and flaky texture.

To store provolone, wrap in aluminum foil or good quality plastic wrap. Store in the refrigerator for several weeks.

Ricotta

Ricotta is actually a by-product of cheese. It's made from the whey of milk that separates from the curds during cheese-making; It is light, delicate, and moist.

Since ricotta is a fresh cheese, it is very perishable. Store fresh ricotta in the refrigerator in a covered container for no more than 2 to 3 days.

Romano

Romano is the oldest cheese of Italy. It is also referred to as Pecorino Romano because it is made from sheep's milk and "pecora" is the Italian word for sheep.

Romano has a granular texture surrounded by a hard, brittle rind. Its flavor ranges from sharp to piquant. It is much sharper than Parmesan cheese and finer when grated.

To store Romano, wrap each piece in aluminum foil or good quality plastic wrap. Store in the refrigerator for several months.

PASTA

Pasta comes in all shapes and sizes. Here is an alphabetical guide to some of the pasta we like to use in our recipes.

Acini de pepe (little peppercorns)

Alphabets (tiny pasta letters)

Anelli (little rings)

Capellini (angel hair pasta)

Cappelletti (nurse's or bishop's caps)

Cavatelli (curled shells)

Conchiglie (medium shells)

Conchigliette (small shells)

Conchiglioni (large shells)

Corrallini (little tubular rings)

Ditalini (tiny thimbles)

Egg noodles (short, flat ribbons)

Elbow macaroni (short, curved pasta tubes)

Elicoidali (ridged, twisted pasta tubes)

Farfalle (bow ties)

Fedelini (round, thin ribbons)

Fettuccine (flat ribbons)

Fettuccine a nido (nested fettuccine)

Fusilli (twisted spaghetti)

Gemelli (double spaghetti twists)

Lasagna noodles (broad pasta ribbons)

Linguine (ribbons)

Mafalda (flat, fluted ribbons)

Mafalda a nido (nested mafalda)

Manicotti (large tubes)

Mostaccioli (smooth pasta tubes)

Orzo or Rosamarina (rice-like pasta)

Penne (short pasta tubes)

Penne rigati (short ridged pasta tubes)

Pennette (tiny, short pasta tubes)

Perciatelli (small tubular macaroni)

Perciatellini (tiny tubular macaroni)

Ravioli (stuffed pillows)

Rigatoni (ridged pasta tubes)

Rotelle (corkscrew macaroni)

Ruote (wagon wheels)

Semi di melone (melon seeds)

Spaetzle (irregular drops of dough)

Spaghetti (round, thin ribbons)

Spaghettini (tiny spaghetti)

Stellini (little stars)

Tortellini (little stuffed pasta twists)

Tripolini (tiny bows)

Tubetti (tiny pasta tubes)

Vermicelli (fine spaghetti)

Ziti (long, tubular macaroni)

Ziti tagliati (cut tubular macaroni)

PASTA COOKING CHART

*F*or 1 pound of pasta, in a dutch oven bring 4 quarts salted water to boiling. If desired, add 1 tablespoon olive oil to help keep the pasta separated while it cooks. Add pasta, a little at a time, so water does not stop boiling. Reduce heat slightly and boil, uncovered, till the pasta is tender but still firm (al dente). Refer to the cooking times below for the particular pasta you are using. Stir occasionally to prevent sticking. When pasta is done, drain in a colander. Serve immediately.

Acini de pepe	4 to 5 minutes
Alphabets	5 to 8 minutes
Anelli	9 to 10 minutes
Capellini	4 to 5 minutes
Cappelletti	9 to 10 minutes
Cavatelli	9 to 10 minutes
Conchiglie	9 to 10 minutes
Conchigliette	8 to 9 minutes
Conchiglioni	9 to 10 minutes
Corrallini	9 to 10 minutes
Ditalini	7 to 9 minutes
Egg noodles	6 to 8 minutes
Elbow macaroni	8 to 10 minutes
Elicoidali	9 to 10 minutes
Farfalle	8 to 10 minutes
Fedelini	7 to 8 minutes
Fettuccine	8 to 10 minutes
Fettuccine a nido	9 to 10 minutes
Fusilli	9 to 10 minutes
Gemelli	8 to 10 minutes
Lasagna noodles	9 to 10 minutes
Linguine	8 to 10 minutes
Mafalda	9 to 10 minutes
Mafalda a nido	9 to 10 minutes
Manicotti	9 to 10 minutes
Mostaccioli	9 to 10 minutes

Orzo or Rosamarina ———————— 5 to 8 minutes
Penne ————————————————— 9 to 10 minutes

Penne rigati —————————————— 9 to 10 minutes
Pennette —————————————————— 8 to 10 minutes
Perciatelli —————————————————— 9 to 10 minutes
Perciatellini ————————————————— 9 to 10 minutes
Ravioli ——————————————————— 9 to 10 minutes
Rigatoni —————————————————— 9 to 10 minutes
Rotelle —————————————————— 8 to 10 minutes
Ruote ——————————————————— 9 to 10 minutes
Semi di melone ——————————————— 5 to 8 minutes
Spaetzle —————————————————— 9 to 10 minutes
Spaghetti —————————————————— 9 to 10 minutes
Spaghettini ————————————————— 8 to 10 minutes
Stellini ——————————————————— 5 to 8 minutes
Tortellini —————————————————— 9 to 10 minutes
Tripolini —————————————————— 5 to 6 minutes
Tubetti ——————————————————— 8 to 10 minutes
Vermicelli —————————————————— 5 to 7 minutes
Ziti ————————————————————— 9 to 10 minutes
Ziti tagliati ————————————————— 9 to 10 minutes

You can order many fine imported Italian ingredients for these recipes from:

Manganaro Foods
488 Ninth Avenue
New York, New York   10018

(212) 563-5331

or toll free 1-800-4SALAMI

NOTES

NOTES

NOTES

NOTES

NOTES

NOTES

NOTES

NOTES

NOTES

NOTES

NOTES